TRIBE OF

Light

How Community Helps Us Heal

ANDREA MICHAL

BALBOA.PRESS

A DIVISION OF HAY HOUSE

Balboa Press books may be ordered through booksellers or by contacting:

Balboa Press
A Division of Hay House
1663 Liberty Drive
Bloomington, IN 47403
www.balboapress.com
844-682-1282

Because of the dynamic nature of the Internet, any web addresses or links contained in this book may have changed since publication and may no longer be valid. The views expressed in this work are solely those of the author and do not necessarily reflect the views of the publisher, and the publisher hereby disclaims any responsibility for them.

The author of this book does not dispense medical advice or prescribe the use of any technique as a form of treatment for physical, emotional, or medical problems without the advice of a physician, either directly or indirectly. The intent of the author is only to offer information of a general nature to help you in your quest for emotional and spiritual well-being. In the event you use any of the information in this book for yourself, which is your constitutional right, the author and the publisher assume no responsibility for your actions.

Any people depicted in stock imagery provided by Getty Images are models, and such images are being used for illustrative purposes only.
Certain stock imagery © Getty Images.

Print information available on the last page.

ISBN: 978-1-9822-6253-2 (sc)
ISBN: 978-1-9822-6255-6 (hc)
ISBN: 978-1-9822-6254-9 (e)

Library of Congress Control Number: 2021901331

Balboa Press rev. date: 03/03/2021

ACKNOWLEDGMENTS

My first thank you is to my wonderful co-authors and collaborators of this book. Without these eight women sharing their heartfelt journeys of healing, <u>Tribe of Light</u> would not be as rich and nourishing as it has become. These exceptional women went through the writing process with grace and then worked with my editor who massaged their stories until they were beautifully expressed works of storytelling art.

I want to share my utmost appreciation for my editor, Shari Hollander. She was essential to this writing process and played a vital role as my sounding board, my go-to sentence and word creator and my friend. She is an amazing editor and person, and I want to honor her greatly for helping me publish this book. I thank her for being my "write-hand woman." I wish her success as she moves forward with her editing career.

And, lastly I want to acknowledge myself. The year 2020 was challenging for everyone and I had much to overcome and learn along the way. I committed to writing <u>Tribe of Light</u> this year, and persevered. I always had my heavenly angels, spirit guides and my father, Leonard Lefitz, by my side. I am proud of the work that I am able to share with others and give to my *community*.

CONTENTS

A Chapter Overview

A Full Circle of Healing
Andrea came full circle after a cancer diagnosis helped her understand that generational and ancestral belief patterns created her illness, and that she ultimately can heal herself with community by her side.

Recovery Through Relationships
"How is your relationship with food like your relationship with people?" asks Jennifer, a certified eating disorder recovery coach. The realization that "staying sick may get me attention but getting well would get me connection" profoundly changed her life.

Soul Moon Rising
After a severe mountain bike accident left her with a traumatic brain injury, Jessica had no choice but to reverse her course and accept help after a lifetime of distancing herself from others, finding her yoga, biking and professional communities as sources of healing.

A Woman's Intuition
An adverse reaction to a bio-identical hormone was Caroline's wake-up call to move herself to the top of her To-Do list and examine what else was toxic in her life. She learned valuable lessons from female elders in Sardinia to handle menopause naturally and aging gracefully.

A Spark of Surrender

A diagnosis of cervical cancer in her thirties left Isolda with two difficult choices: give life or keep her own life. Her poignant story reveals how she learned the art of surrender and absolute trust on her path.

Finding the True Me

What if you were angry at God and had lost your faith after a loved one passed away? Barbara's spiritual journey after loss and grief was key to her being able to give back and help her community heal after 9/11.

Rooted in Faith

Mira learned that it's not just a "place" that makes you feel safe. Belonging to a community with shared religious beliefs and planting your spiritual "roots" helps you belong anywhere.

Infinite Wisdom from Our Ocean Family

After suffering the heartbreak of losing two horses following a divorce, Heather's special connection to the ocean helped her come out of isolation as she followed her intuition—and heart—into a new community where her career flourishes.

A Quest for Belonging that Brought Me Home

Catheryne understands that community is an intricate network of individuals, inextricably linked across space and time, that shapes our collective experience and brings us home.

INTRODUCTION

"We are human because we belong. We are made for community, for togetherness, for family to exist in a delicate network of interdependence."

- Bishop Desmond Tutu, Nobel Peace Prize Winner

I was inspired to learn that in certain regions of South Africa, when someone does something wrong, that person is taken to the center of the village and surrounded by their tribe. For two days, the tribe speaks of all the good that this person has done. The tribe believes that each person is inherently good, yet sometimes makes mistakes, which is really a cry for help. They unite in this ritual to encourage the person to reconnect with his or her true nature. The belief is that unity and affirmation have more power to change behavior than shame and punishment. This is known as *Ubuntu*, "I am because we are." This example of community exemplifies the idea that we are all interdependent and when we recognize this co-existent relationship, we are able to lift each other's spirits as we lift our own.

Tribe of Light, How Community Helps Us Heal, is a compilation of stories from transformational coaches, therapists and other healing practitioners. These nine women share their truth, wisdom and lessons of how community helped them HEAL through difficulties and challenges in their own lives. I am honored to have collaborated with these amazing women who recognize their humanness on their path of remembrance and wholeness. As referenced in my last book, Beacon of Light, 14 Keys to Unlock the Light Within You, we are all like empty canvasses, and just as the creation of art, we change, transform and become beautiful masterpieces of timeless existence. Community is an important part of this transformational process. We need each other as reflections of ourselves, so that we can SEE and GROW into what we truly are… magnificent essences of light and love.

Everyone experiences their journey differently. These stories will give you a glimpse into how community interactions and connections have shaped the lives of these contributing writers. Our hope is <u>Tribe of Light</u> will give you some insight into your own personal journey as well.

Community. When we break down this word, we find UNITY in it. Yes, as the saying goes, "We are in this together." We are meant to recognize the beauty in each other as individuals and the remarkable UNIT we are too. Our collective experiences and challenges that we face in our every day lives teach us to value each other with compassion and empathy.

The world cannot continue to be separated and torn apart. It is time we understand that we are an integral part of each other. Whether our time is spent more alone in our introspection, or with a group of people, we must open our eyes to the understanding that we are all connected.

Our planet and everything on it is bound by an invisible connection between people, animals, plants, trees, the air, the water, and the soil. Actions on our part, whether positive or negative, can have an impact on people and the environment. Staying conscious of the connection between all things can help us think of our choices and our life in terms of the broader effect we may be creating.

My wish for you, as you read this book, is to have an open heart as you delve into your own healing process and reflect on how the interconnection of all of us – and within your personal communities - plays a role in your decisions and natural state of well-being.

With gratitude,
Andrea

A FULL CIRCLE OF HEALING

By Andrea Michal

"True healing means drawing the circle of our being larger and becoming more inclusive, more capable of loving. In this sense, healing is not for the sick alone, but for all humankind.

- Richard Moss, Author

Patterns. Wounds. Trauma. We all have them to conquer

Awakening and shifting our old belief systems is what we humans are doing on Earth at this time. Remembering who we truly are as light beings, becoming more whole, actualized, or embodied and understanding the enormous capacity for unconditional love of ourselves and each other.

Through my writing, I dare to be vulnerable and share my stories because I believe we can all find healing and strength through storytelling. The truth for me is that when I read or listen to other people share their life experiences, as challenging or uplifting as they may be, I understand I am not alone. We are in this healing process together. We have unique paths; but in the end, we need each other to get through the tough times, and our connection with one another is crucial to our overall well-being.

Letting go of worry

I was told my paternal grandmother died of colon cancer. I never met her because, tragically, she passed away in her 50s, before I was born. My father, her youngest son, also had colon cancer in his late

60s. He underwent major surgery to remove part of his colon, called a re-section. Gratefully, he recovered and lived more than 20 years after his diagnosis until he died of an unrelated illness in his early 80s. I miss him each day and think lovingly of him and the life experiences he and my mother provided for me and my two brothers and his grandchildren.

So, I knew I needed to have a colonoscopy at 50. I made an appointment. I went under anesthesia and woke up an hour later, groggy and a bit disoriented. All good they told me. Whew! I had dodged the proverbial bullet.

A reprieve of five years until I had to think about it again. At 55, I would be due for another colonoscopy; you know: out of sight, out of mind. I was living life with passion, traveling around the world, dancing, playing, and working intentionally through my days, and it was really good. I realized that I'd let the deadline pass—I was now 57—and I knew I needed to schedule a colonoscopy once again. I decided to go before the end of the year, not because I had any concerns, but because it was December and I wanted to use my 2019 insurance deductible. My practical decision turned out to be a lifesaver. Call it "Divine timing" or "my angels having my back."

I woke up after this colonoscopy and heard the doctor telling me these heart-dropping words, "It's very small, but it's there." Let me assure you "very small" does not reduce the fear caused by these loaded words "You will have to take care of it," as the doctor proceeded to tell me. Instantly, I felt the initial shock wave of disbelief, then came denial. My thoughts were "It's got to be a mistake." It can't be cancer. Oh, shit (literally)—I was leaving for a two-week trip out of the country in five days!

As I left the surgery center, my eyes filled with tears. I said to myself, what more could happen in the year 2019? What a year it had been for me on so many levels. Personal growth was evident by the significant changes in my life and inner workings. Everyone was celebrating the year end. People were saying that 2019 was the hardest year of their lives. Who would have thought that the new year, 2020, would be another exceptional year of "healing" through chaos, conflict and challenge? Among other things, 2020 will be known as a time of collective healing rather than just individual transformation; both happening simultaneously, focusing not only on the self, but on our community, country and the entire world.

I always was a person who "beat to her own drum," so to speak, so I never took my health for granted. For the last 10 years and presently, I chose a diet that was different from my family of origin's, consuming mostly organic, plant-based food. I also eat various superfoods and take amazing supplements. I nourish myself with probiotics for good gut health; exercise everyday with yoga, tennis and walking or hiking; and I work on my mental, emotional, and spiritual health with meditation, coaching, reading, writing and journaling. How could this cancer diagnosis have happened to *me*?

Our present societal beliefs assume that a genetic or pre-disposed illness shows itself in our physical form because it is passed down from generation to generation. Reading this, maybe you're thinking: "Your cancer diagnosis was unavoidable because it was genetic." Perhaps. But I want to explain my belief that, sometimes, an illness manifests in the body if the triggers are stress related, not only because they are passed down "genetically" or through heredity. So, if an individual reacts to situations with stress or carries unconscious or undo stress, the illness that is associated with a family history, such as cancer, may actually arise and present itself more imminently. I have seen and experienced how illness can be eradicated if the "source" of the stress is understood more clearly within the context of our mind, body and spirit connection. This mind, body and spirit connection is vital for all of us to understand, for it is a powerful tool and the KEY to helping the healing process.

There is a commonly held belief that there's nothing we can do about illness but treat it and hope it goes away. We now know that changing our diet, exercise routines and other physical rituals can prevent our illnesses from becoming worse or create better outcome for our health. But what if we can change our patterns, trauma and behaviors that were passed down to us? Could there be more to healing an illness rather than giving up and/or using the conventional remedies and procedures?

Throughout my life, I have witnessed how the mind, body and spirit are intertwined. Therefore, I decided to dive more deeply into

3

the possibilities of how I could have manifested this disease inside of MY BODY. How could I heal this ancestral and generational illness? Intuitively, I knew it was time to clear the old patterns that may have caused the colon cancer. I felt in my heart and soul that it absolutely must not be passed down to the next generation—my three sons. Could I do it? Could I end a pattern that had been carried from generation to generation?

As I wrote in my previous books, the word "dis-ease" means we are "not at ease" with ourselves. Illness, I have come to understand, is mostly created from a part of us that is not content or at peace within. I'd come to believe, through my own therapy, introspection, reflection and observing my reactions, that in my case, my "dis-ease" was caused by WORRY. I worried a great deal, more than I realized. Looking at my life, I could see how worry was an overwhelming source of anxiety for me. I'd worry whether or not my suitcase would come off the conveyor belt at the airport when I traveled. I worried that any one of my sons would be in a car accident when they drove anywhere. I worried about whether or not I'd be successful in my (future) coaching career. I worried about relationships and my health. And I worried considerably about the world and the challenging times we are in. I worried from a micro-level to a macro, or global, perspective.

Even when I wasn't consciously aware of it, worry ran at an unconscious depth inside of me like a current under the surface of a flowing river. Not because I wanted to worry, but because my family patterning ran through my cells. Being born Jewish, worry was a survival instinct. Existentially, my family accumulated patterns of worry, not only from generations upon generations, but from thousands of years of persecution.

The Jewish people have a stereotypical but legitimate history of worry, both for their personal safety and as a way of measuring their value in society. Are we doing well? How can we do better? Why is this happening to us? Are we too visible? Are we visible enough? What can we do to change it? Worry, worry, worry. All the time, worry. Worry became a coping mechanism that was ingrained in me, culturally, genetically and as a pattern of extreme self-protection.

I can now tell you the story of my recovery; how I dislodged the pattern of worry, removed the cancer, and truly found how community was part of my healing process along the way. I was determined to heal myself from the inside out. I happen to be a strong-willed and tenacious woman, so I decided to go a different route with the illness that lay before me. I would still travel, put the illness away in my mind for the time being, and stay in a calm space so I could receive any guidance I needed from the people around me and my spirit guides as well. I would be traveling for two weeks; first, to the city of San Miguel de Allende in Mexico, where the spirit of Archangel Michael, the leader of all the archangels and the Angel of Protection, is present; then to the jungles of Costa Rica, where I would immerse myself in a detox with foods, clean water and self-reflection. What better time to embark on a journey to cleanse my soul and work on letting go of the worry that had been with me for my lifetime and the many generations before me.

In December, I serendipitously received an email from a natural healing center in Costa Rica asking me to run retreats there. I perused their website and the words "Wild Leadership" caught my eye. Instead of facilitating a "Re-Wild You" retreat (as I do here in the United States for women), I decided to join this retreat as a participant. I was pleasantly surprised. I met a beautiful tribe of 50 like-minded people in Costa Rica. You see, we came together to be on this Wild Leadership Retreat with a local facilitator and global leader who taught us Quantum Energy techniques to give us a new level of vibrancy and power. I practiced these energy modalities at the expansive beaches and breathtakingly magnificent waterfalls surrounding me. I also practiced breathwork and meditation with all kinds of monkeys and birds chattering noisily in the jungle. I still use the tools that I learned on this retreat today, and I apply the concepts of prayer, meditation and "mind over matter" to heal my body in any circumstances that are present. In these awe-inspiring Costa Rican surroundings, I reflected on the concept of "letting go"—of not controlling the outcome of all of my experiences, and trusting the Universe, God and my higher self, more deeply. I knew, though, that the cancer had to be removed. Not only for my physical health, but also for the metaphorical "removal" of the worry from my spirit, for the healing of generations to come.

When I returned home, I encountered much community support from hundreds of people in my life, not only through my social media platforms, but also from my personal friends, family and co-workers. I was surrounded by love. I am blessed. I believe I was being watched over by my angels and spirit guides the entire time. In fact, I believe we are all watched over by our guides at all times. I was keenly aware that every part of my travel and community experiences were divinely orchestrated for me. My medical process was truly magical. I found amazing doctors and surgeons at one of the best hospitals in Los Angeles. I felt confident that I was going to have a full recovery. And I was right. I was playing tennis and snow skiing within six weeks of my surgery.

Again, my tribe at home was continuous in their love and devotion, and I felt nourished by them in every way. I had visits in the hospital (even a party in my room the afternoon of New Year's Eve) and I was cared for as I recovered from the five-hour surgery that I had undergone. I realized that although many healing journeys are personal ones, the community's support and compassion creates an important "container" or "holds the space" for healing to occur on an even greater level. This experience inspired me to collaborate and create this book. I also had another "aha" moment within this particular journey. I know that I am a *giver*. Most women are. This experience created a new pathway for me to become a *receiver* as well. I had little opportunity to be the giver in this situation, so I allowed myself to receive. It was a lovely surprise to see how many people wanted to comfort me and bring nourishing food or just sit by my side. I truly embraced the idea of being attended to and I then understood how community was a source of unwavering support for me.

As I write this opening chapter, it has now been many months since the surgery, and I am completely clear of cancer; no further treatment was needed. While I may be concerned about situations in my life, I am *liberated* from the underlying worry and fear about the outcome of my experiences. I now practice *discernment* when I need to make a decision, rather than operating from a place of anxiety. I appreciate this change in me.

Although the social and political climate are extremely heightened at the time of this writing, I am able to be calm with the state of the world around me. I experience joy in my life every day and I react to situations with clarity. Identifying and healing the generational and ancestral patterns within my family has helped me remove my state of anxiety and worry. I believe my sons will embrace my new perspective on life and see me as a role-model through my actions and behaviors. It is important to note that we can all heal ourselves, and *community is essential in this healing process*. And, when we heal ourselves, the patterns are broken, and we can then be of true service to others.

In my case, the transformation of my old patterns eradicated the recurrence of my illness and it ceased to exist. With this change, the next generations have the opportunity to have a new outcome; one of blessings of good health and well-being. This experience will then become a full circle of healing for everyone.

Andrea Michal is an Author, Intuitive, Holistic Life Coach and Mentor who shares her wisdom to educate and transform her clients through one-on-one private sessions, her inspiring workshops and The MasterSoul Program™. Her gift for gentle coaching creates a safe space for deeper expression and insight. Her empathy and compassion reassure clients that they have the opportunity to overcome challenges with ease and grace. Andrea is also an entrepreneur, philanthropist and the proud mother of three talented young men. She spends her time between Westlake Village and Ojai, where she finds joy and peace in the beauty of those tranquil California communities.

www.AndreaMichal.com

RECOVERY THROUGH RELATIONSHIPS

By Jennifer Mullaney

"Life isn't about waiting for the storm to pass...it's about learning to dance in the rain."

- Vivian Greene, author

Eating disorders can be cunning, deceptive, and sly. Mine kept me and my family in denial for years. However, in January 2005, at the age of 19, it had become alarmingly apparent that my relationship to food and exercise had spiraled out of control. My grades plummeted first semester sophomore year of college. My roommate refused to live with me until I got the treatment I desperately needed. And, finally, I was hospitalized over winter break to stabilize my weight and vitals. I had to face the fact that something needed to change. What I didn't realize was that there was a correlation between my relationship with food and my relationship with people.

As early as I can remember, I craved reassurance and validation from others. All I ever wanted was to be seen, to feel special. This was paired with an extremely strong will and a temperament that both served me well *and* led to self-destruction. In <u>8 Keys to Recovery from an Eating Disorder</u>, the authors explain how certain personality traits can be either assets or liabilities. At best, I was precise, thorough, high-energy, and determined. These traits kept me excelling academically, involved in various extracurricular activities, and out of trouble. At worst, these same traits caused me to be perfectionistic, obsessive, anxious, and stubborn. My traits, when not channeled in the right direction, brought about panic attacks, difficulty connecting with peers, and kept me entrapped in the chains of an eating disorder. I had learned to derive my sense of self-worth and specialness not from *who I was*, but rather from the *things that I did*— grades, awards, miles run, calories consumed, a number on a scale. These were the things I was praised for; so, naturally, they were also the things I'd come to value. And yet, I still felt empty. No matter how well I did in school, how much I improved in dance, or how much weight I lost, it never felt like enough.

People often ask me how I recovered from an eating disorder. It's a valid question. Eating disorders have the highest mortality rate of any mental illness. While I received treatment at a state-of-the-art residential facility staffed with leading professionals who took an individualized approach, not everyone I went to treatment with recovered. Some are still in their eating disorders, and sadly, some have died. So, what distinguishes those who recover from those who don't? Without hesitation, I always respond: *relationships*. For me, there was a turning point when engaging in the relationships I valued became more important than engaging in my eating disorder behaviors. That's not to diminish the fact that recovery was the hardest thing I have ever done in my entire life, but relationships became the glue that held my progress together. They were the "why" that kept me trudging forward even when it felt impossible to keep going.

As much as I needed to learn how to receive food, I also needed to learn how to receive people. This didn't occur to me until I was given the assignment: *How is your relationship with food like your relationship with people?* I knew that I needed food to heal. As much as I resisted it, that part made sense. But I rejected the notion that I needed people to get better. People were unpredictable, unreliable, scary. How could I ever trust people? The only person I ever dared to rely on was myself, but that faux independence nearly killed me. It landed me in a treatment center where I was forced to put my life on pause and assess what got me there. I didn't trust the food and I most certainly didn't trust my body's ability to eat and/or keep it. And, as I started to write the assignment, I discovered that my thoughts and feelings, particularly fear, about food were in alignment with my thoughts and feelings about people.

My relationship with food mirrored my relationship with people. I couldn't remember the last time I sat down at a table with others, ate, and kept my food. It was not only unfamiliar, it was terrifying. I didn't want to need the food in front of me and I most certainly didn't want to need these people around me. The same way I was afraid that one bite of a brownie would take over me and lead me to devour the entire pan and have to purge, I was convinced letting another human being in would cause me to forsake any sense of agency I had. It would necessitate complete and utter reliance, reverting me to a permanently dependent state. A state where I would be left vulnerable to constant disappointment, scrutiny, and rejection by others. I was certain that my emotional needs were too great to be met. I wanted brownies and connection, but I thought others would ridicule and fear me if they knew just how deeply I wanted either. My emotional hunger scared me even more than my physical hunger. Ironically, the two things that terrified me the most, food and people, were ultimately the things that would heal me.

One of the first people I met in treatment was my primary therapist. What she lacked in height, she made up for in energy, intensity, and hair volume. She had piercing blue eyes that I couldn't look into without feeling completely vulnerable and exposed. I hid my terror by putting up a tough front. In one of our first sessions, she asked me, "Jenny, what do you have to live for?" I was adamant, "I have NOTHING to live for and I don't care if I die." But she wasn't one to back down. Thankfully, I was assigned to a therapist just as strong-willed as me, so she pressed, "There has to be someone or something you enjoy or feel passionate about. Family? Friends? School? Wouldn't you like to get back to Berkeley?" Little did she know, my home life was a disaster. Get better for my family?! More like, get as far away from that shit show as possible. I felt like my friends were all so repulsed by my behavior over the past few years that they had no emotional bandwidth left for me. And, I absolutely hated Berkeley. I didn't want to go back. In fact, in retrospect, I believe one of the functions of my eating disorder was a silent protest against ending up there after high school.

I didn't have the words to articulate how small my life felt or how hopeless I was at the time, so the therapist and I sat in silence, at a standstill, her eyes making me feel even more uncomfortable than usual. I had to break the tension with something; she wasn't going to let this go. So, I whispered, "I sort of like to dance." The dance studio was one of my earliest experiences of community. A return to that, at a time I felt estranged from myself and others, would be highly therapeutic. Dance was a safe haven for me as a child. It was an escape from family tension, an outlet for my emotions, and a way to avoid family dinners. And, yes, while that last one may have become problematic once I started using it as a way to hide eating disorder behaviors, it also helped protect me from the toxicity brewing in my household.

I grew up dancing competitively and it was my dream to pursue dance professionally after high school. However, my parents did not support this endeavor. I was a straight-A student, valedictorian of my high school class, with an off-the-charts SAT score in math. I wasn't permitted to waste my intellect on a pipe dream, like dancing professionally. In order to acquiesce to my parent's expectations, I decided that I would attend UCLA. That way I could go to school while being close to the professional dance scene. But when I was accepted to UC Berkeley and not UCLA, that dream went down the drain. I couldn't handle the disappointment of working so hard and it still not being enough to get me what I wanted. In near-perfect synchronicity with that major let down, I clung to the pseudo-security of my eating disorder to cope.

My therapist jumped on this kernel of information like it was gold, and so did the rest of the staff. The clinical director came in with a flyer about Disney auditions. Another therapist brought in tap shoes for all of the clients and used Monday night creativity group as an opportunity for us to dance. One of the staff took every opportunity to talk to me about her work as a producer in the professional dance world. I had a group of people rallying around me, supporting a dream I had all but given up on—my dream of being a professional dancer.

As I sit here writing about it, I'm filled with so much emotion. The staff didn't just treat the *patient*; they were treating the *person*. Strangely, this individualized care filled me with an overwhelming sense of sadness. In some ways it was even more painful to take in their love and support than it was to take in the food. Finding community in eating disorder treatment brought me face to face with the lack of connection I had in my immediate family. For the first time ever, I felt completely seen and unconditionally accepted, even in the moments I was a mess—and there were many. It was unlike anything I'd ever felt in my entire life. I was experiencing a caliber of love, support, and validation that my parents never provided for me, not because they didn't love me, but because it was outside their emotional intelligence. It was something I was going to have to grieve if I wanted to get well. I began to realize, that while they would always be my family, they weren't a part of what I now know is my *tribe*.

I was terrified to live life without my eating disorder, but I was even more terrified of going back to Berkeley, or worse, to my parents' house. The thought of leaving the first place to ever really feel like home and losing the people who made it feel that way was more painful than the thought of leaving my eating disorder behind. The relationships I was forming were becoming more significant than the eating disorder. My eating disorder didn't like this. It got louder. It would say things like: *These people are only being nice to you because they are getting paid. They don't really care about you. No one does. You are nothing without me. You aren't special. Once you leave treatment, you will never see them again. They are making you weak. You are going to leave here NEEDING them, but you will have NO ONE! You are going to need me if you want to dance professionally. You are going to be so fat when you get out of here, you will get laughed out of dance class.* It was relentless, so I started to talk about these thoughts in individual and group sessions.

I reluctantly made the choice to trust the people around me, anchoring to the staff and clients instead of my eating disorder. This took a level of vulnerability and authenticity deeper than I had ever shown up with in relationships. Connecting with others satiated the emotional hunger pangs that neither eating disorder behaviors nor food could quell. This was about so much more than the food. It was then that I realized—staying sick may get me *attention* but getting well would get me *connection*.

Eating disorder treatment didn't just challenge my beliefs about food, it challenged my beliefs about people. The connections I made in treatment did not cease to exist after I was well enough to graduate from residential. I went on to live at the transitional living house, which provided a place where the work of reintegrating into the real world and building a life outside of treatment happened, while still having the support of staff and others in my same situation. I have come to call them all my *soul sisters*, the first members of my tribe. I maintained existing relationships and new ones blossomed. My eating disorder was wrong and realizing this helped the healthy voice inside of me grow stronger. The *community* I cultivated during treatment gave me the tools to recreate it in new places as I ventured out into the world.

The first place I ventured outside of treatment was the professional dance world. I remember feeling so intimidated by the dancers and teachers, but I kept showing up—just like I had to in treatment. Soon, I became a familiar face at the EDGE, and in spite of near debilitating surges of social anxiety, I chose to be brave. I started staying after class to socialize with other dancers and teachers. Before long, I was getting invited to happy hours, performances, parties and I signed with my first dance agent. I found community in the dance world. I didn't want to be the weird girl who wasn't eating or running to the bathroom after sharing a meal with friends. I'd rather stay, be present, and engage in the table talk. Showing up in this way, as I had learned from my treatment experience, made me a magnet for genuine, kind, authentic people.

I was presented with another opportunity to create community in the real world when I got a job at Starbucks. One of my coworkers came from an Italian family who owned a catering business in New Jersey. She grew up in a family that embraced the pleasure of cooking and eating together. My friend had such a positive, healthy, balanced relationship with food and her body. Though I had experienced this with the staff who treated me, it was refreshing and almost shocking to find someone in the "outside" world who did. She was exactly the kind of person with whom I could recreate the food practices I established in treatment. When I told her about my history and some of my lingering food fears, she was supportive and saw it as an opportunity to explore and support me on my journey. She cooked so many amazing meals for me, and we would go out to eat frequently. We turned my food fears into a game of firsts. I ate so many foods I hadn't had since before my eating disorder. We are still friends to this day; she too, is part of my tribe.

My community expanded even more when I started teaching dance at various children's studios. I felt an instant love and connection with my students, and their parents were always generous. I was showered with gifts, home-cooked meals, and invitations to family gatherings. It gave me the same sense of family I felt as a child at my own dance studio. I was in early recovery, but I knew I wanted to be a positive role model for my students. They were growing up in a diet culture, bombarded with unrealistic images of bodies, participating in a physically demanding activity that, until recently, had a narrow range of acceptable body types. It was no coincidence that I was working in a place that could potentially be a breeding ground for eating disorders. I chose to use it as an opportunity to empower my students by shifting the focus away from body aesthetics and placing emphasis on all the amazing things they could train their bodies to do. I knew I couldn't just *talk the talk*; I had to *walk the walk* if I wanted to make a real impact. There were instances in recovery where I would struggle with an eating disorder thought or urge and my healthy self would chime in asking: *What would you want for one of your students?*

My healing process wasn't linear. Sometimes it felt like one step forward, three steps back. In early recovery, I struggled with occasional purging and a few isolated incidents of self-harm. I found myself in a toxic relationship with a man who made comments about my body that mirrored the eating disorder voice. And my weight did some pendulum swings below and above my body's natural set point. But I would show up to therapy, reach out to a trusted friend, or attend an alumni group to anchor back into the community that helped me heal in the first place. For every slip-up, I stood up once more until there were no more slip-ups to be had.

Fifteen years later, I consider myself fully recovered from my eating disorder and have been for several years. In <u>100 Questions & Answers</u>

<u>About Eating Disorders</u>, Carolyn Costin defines recovered as: Being recovered is when the person can accept his or her natural body size and shape and no longer has a self-destructive relationship with food or exercise. When you are recovered, food and weight take a proper perspective in your life and what you weigh is not more important than who you are; in fact, actual numbers are of little or no importance at all. When recovered, you will not compromise your health or betray your soul to look a certain way, wear a certain size, or reach a certain number on the scale. When you are recovered, you do not use eating disorder behaviors to deal with, distract from, or cope with other problems.

I have a better relationship now with food, exercise, and my body than most people who have never even had an eating disorder. And while I no longer have eating disorder thoughts or urges, *relationships* are still my "why" for so many things. They are a motivating force. They give my life meaning.

I witness the healing power of relationships in the work I now do as an eating disorder recovery coach. I see a definitive shift happen when a client starts turning to people instead of their eating disorder. When clients start reaching out to me instead of behaviors, they are more apt to challenge food fears, and their healthy self gets stronger even in the moments I'm not there. They say things like, "I was at the grocery store this weekend and asked myself, 'What would Jen have me do?'" and "Our connection is motivation for me to get better because I want to be on the other side with you." One of my clients absolutely blossomed when she took an art class. She quickly connected with her peers and took huge strides forward in her recovery. Initially, she turned to me instead of her eating disorder and, with the new-found confidence she had in our connection, she was able to go out into the world and connect with others. She found community, as I once did, and it is helping her heal.

Life without an eating disorder, fully recovered, creates space, time, and energy for relationships, adventures, and opportunities I never dreamed possible. I get to live from a place of love and bravery rather than fear. Putting this into action, I recently decided to take an all-female stand-up comedy class called *Pretty, Funny Women*. The thought of doing stand-up comedy equally terrified and excited me. At the beginning of each class, we went around the room, reporting our comedy wins to the rest of the group. My wins for the week would always include who I hung out with from the class. Because for me, no matter what I accomplish or achieve, the connections I make are always the biggest win. By the end of the 8 weeks, I had spent time with every student and the teaching assistant outside of class time. In a phone conversation after the showcase, my teacher commented, "Jenny, you are talented. You are a hustler. You are a light in this world and people love you." I was stunned. She noticed parts of me that I wasn't even trying to present, things that had nothing to do with comedy. I was simply showing up as myself, fully and authentically. I'm so grateful and touched by her words of affirmation, not only because she saw who I was so clearly in a short time, but because I was finally in a mind-set and heart space to fully receive them.

There is a power in being able to receive from a place of being whole. The more clearly I see and witness myself, the more open I am to be seen and validated by others. And every time I do, it's as if the little girl inside of me, who just wanted so badly to be seen and feel special, is finally able to receive it as well. I receive people with gratitude and delight, just as I do food, money, sex, and all of life's pleasures. Showing up for myself in this way, as a whole person, without guilt or shame and allowing myself to fully receive, is what fuels my consistent ability to show up for others.

My tribe is vast, comprising beautiful souls from childhood, treatment, dance, teaching, school, travel, Starbucks, serving jobs, stand-up, social events, mutual friends, and kismet encounters. While it is an eclectic mix of people, they all have one thing in common. Members of my tribe give me the same feeling of *home*—unconditional love, stability, safety, security. And no matter how much time passes between talks on the phone or face-to-face encounters, our love and connection transcend that space and time. I wouldn't have found my tribe without eating disorder treatment because I wouldn't have even known to look for it. The staff and soul sisters from treatment gave me a feeling of home I didn't even know I was missing until I felt it for the first time fifteen years ago. They created a safe space for me to strip away the armor of my eating disorder and find what was buried deep underneath—sensitivity, kindness, compassion, and resilience. I discovered an infinite capacity to love and be loved, an innate source of light for myself and others, and an unprecedented ability to heal. Being brave enough to relinquish my armor and surrender is the thing of which I am most proud. And what I uncovered are the things that truly make me special.

Jennifer Mullaney is a certified eating disorder recovery coach through the Carolyn Costin Institute since 2018. She is also a certified reiki practitioner and dance teacher. She resides in Calabasas, California, with her dog and cat.

www.recoveredispossible.com

SOUL MOON RISING

By Jessica Julian

"Give up all questions except one: "Who am I?" After all, the only fact you are sure of is that you are."

- Sri Nisargadatta Maharaj

I was born under a full moon in 1973 on a May evening in Seattle, Washington. At my birth, it was *Luna* who brought light to the first inhale of my life...*Luna* who illuminated the sounds of my first exhale. Cries of separation and aloneness that would eventually become the song I was most comfortable singing.

This particular full moon in May is known as the Buddha Moon (*Buddha* means "awakened one"). Stories from Buddhism say the Buddha himself was born, became enlightened—or awakened—and died under this May full moon. The Buddha Moon has continued to illuminate my life, while specific Buddhist teachings—The Three Jewels—have supported me in fully participating in my living. These Three Jewels are the *Buddha*, the *Dharma*, and the *Sangha*—the Teacher, the Teachings, and the Community. These principles have guided me and helped me accept that we are not wired to walk this path alone.

1) **The Buddha: one who is awakened to their true nature, the potentiality in all beings.**

As an only child from a long ancestral line of women who aligned with wildness and wolves, I've always been solitary and a little unusual. From about the age of six, I spent hours alone in the forests surrounding my house, serving mud pies to imaginary friends who came in the form of insects, reptiles, and the abundant Pacific Northwest greenery. It was there, deep amongst the trees, that I felt most at home because the actual environment I lived in was often unpredictable, depressing, lonely, and sometimes violent. In the woods, the trees provided comfort, and one beautiful pine became my favorite reading spot. To feel closer to a God I had not learned about formally but felt as a calm experience, I would climb her limbs almost to the top and feel her breathe into me. Allowing myself to relax back into the vanilla-scented bark with her branches wrapped around me, I imagined these as the arms of the wise and loving mother I prayed mine would to turn into. At this young age, I would sit and ponder who I was, what the meaning of life was, and why my soul was here on this Earth. I wrestled with the fear of growing older because it seemed like a death of my essence and joy. The adults in my life seemed devoid of real breath, lacking vitality, like withered and barren branches hanging from a lifeless tree. This left me afraid that I, too, would forget these sacred moments in the tree that reminded me I was part of a larger existence. This early fear shifted into a guiding sense of life purpose that I desperately wanted to continue to remember myself. And still today, 40 years later, when I have those moments of almost forgetting, I turn to Mother Nature, to the trees, and I feel *her*, that continuous line of soul running throughout my life. This is where remembering and presence meet, and where my own root system has deepened enough for me to grow wings.

2) **The Dharma: the teachings that awaken the true nature of love and understanding in all beings.**

The years of life and time moved on. I remained close in relationship with nature and my existential nomadic seeking. However, I continued to carry with me the fear of forgetting who I was, which kept me lying awake at night. Yet, the longing for connection with others began to stir and grow as I reached adulthood. I was a chameleon who could *fit in* anywhere but acutely felt the absence of *belonging*. At nineteen, I began visiting different churches, thinking religion might fill that existential void, but it only justified the feeling that I didn't belong. A few years later, I found yoga and, for the first time, a *community* that helped me access a similar space of connection within myself that I previously had only found in nature. I delved into the spiritual teachings of form, meditation, breath, and philosophy, which initially helped my healing process. Eventually, though, it became a Band-Aid on the deeper psychological wounds I was carrying around.

In 2000, I became a yoga teacher and continued to study with one of my mentors who was rooted in Buddhist psychology. I was immediately drawn to this systematic approach of understanding and working with my own mind and experienced a gradual increase of students reaching out, seeking support for ways to work with their own minds and to relieve their suffering. At that same time, I embarked on a journey of psychotherapy with a Jungian analyst. When the private yoga sessions began to feel more like therapy, I entered a graduate program in psychology, which lead to a second profession as a licensed marriage and family therapist. Despite my life of honest self-inquiry, psycho-spiritual growth, and a community found in both the worlds of yoga and psychology, I continued to keep myself on the fringes of the pack, entering and leaving on my own terms. A sense of independence and safety, yes; but also a looming shadow of loneliness, questioning *what is it that heals one towards true wholeness?*

3) **The Sangha: A community of supportive others who come together in harmony and awareness; a place to help and be helped by.**

Years of working with poses, meditation techniques, psychological awareness, and spiritual inquiry did not prepare me for a life-changing moment on June 12, 2010. I'd had a particularly difficult day as a psychology intern and came home to clear my inner space by getting into the mountains on my bike. There is something incredibly healing in the way the wind blows swiftly across my face as my bike glides freely downhill. Within an hour, all the angst of the day's material dissipated in the uphill climb of my familiar trail. By the time I got to the top, I was feeling expansive and clear headed. I paused to drink in the rolling hills and wide-open space with no one around and said to myself, "I am so lucky to be alive. My life is such a blessing. This is God's country." Although I have no current memory of it, just two minutes later while pedaling full speed downhill, I was knocked immediately unconscious from the impact of my head hitting the rocky slope.

When I came back to consciousness, I was midway through a phone call, blood dripping from my face, and feeling completely disoriented. Any familiarity of the trail was wiped from my brain during the traumatic impact. A strong, supportive *presence* (and I am sure many pain-releasing chemicals from my brain) gave me the ability to get back on my damaged bike and ride three miles to the end of the trail where I had help waiting to take me to the emergency room. That evening I underwent two hours of facial reconstructive surgery, X-rays, CAT scans, and countless hours of wound cleaning and tending. Eventually I was sent home, visually unrecognizable and diagnosed with a traumatic brain injury, to begin the long journey of understanding and healing.

All of the self-care techniques and inner resources I had spent a lifetime gathering were of limited use in the first few months of healing and during the following year, which consisted of three more surgeries (two more on my face, one on my hand). In those moments, there was certainly not a yoga pose that could help, a specific meditation technique that seemed appropriate, or even a philosophy book I could pick up to make me instantly feel better. Talk therapy was of no use, as my mouth and face were stitched up to hold together the remaining tissues until they could heal and grow back on their own. The only thing I could do was allow myself to be completely present, breathe, and witness the incredible healing powers that these actions had on my physical body. All of my doctors were astonished at the rapid rate of my recovery and constantly asked what it was that I was doing to heal so quickly. Of course, I was blessed with good health prior to the accident; but my answer was always consistent and clear: "I'm just deeply breathing, and I have so much loving support around me."

Before the mountain bike accident in 2010, there was a drive within me, a hunger of sorts, to claim complete self-reliance and drive out any need to belong or depend on another. I was resistant to asking for help; perfectionism permeated everything I touched, as if there were someone or something I needed to prove myself to. I rode my bike alone as fast as I could, blasting loud rock music through my earphones while in the public eye, hid softly behind the teachings on compassion and community, never fully allowing myself to truly BE in it. Internally, I was deeply suffering from the ways I was not truly belonging to myself, which kept me separate from others. In reflection, so much of my healing has come from the support and love of the friends and connections I've made through the yoga, psychology, and biking communities. People who have shared their words, their hearts, their healing food and their time with me. Beautiful individuals who were simply inviting me to belong, exactly as I already was.

"What you seek is seeking you." -St Francis

It is night now, nearly 10 years after the bike accident, and I sit silently, and gratefully,
listening....
to the warm wind moving through the trees,
to the dirt shifting beneath the exhale of my body dropping down like
     a root.
to the yearly spring symphony of the frogs and the night birds.
to my heart that lives in these mountains, in nature, my home.
I breathe in.
Each inhale, the sound of my Spirit soaring in the spaciousness of the
     nightly skies.
Years of seeking and striving has led me to this, to where I've always been;
Free in my refuge of solitude and with the peace that only aloneness
     can bring.
I look up and see her, *Luna,* my May Buddha moon, shining brightly
     like a jewel.
She reminds me of our history together and whispers sweetly
"there's more, dear one, keep awakening"
I inhale deeper as she illuminates the beauty of my life in this moment.
One already flowing freely between connection and aloneness.

My life now with no more seeking, nothing more to know.
A life simply waiting for me to step into it, to what is already here.
("keep awakening" she whispers)
I Exhale and know....
my life, my community, my whole self,
right here, right now.

Jessica Julian is a licensed marriage and family therapist in California specializing in trauma and wellness who has also been teaching yoga and mindfulness since 2000. Jessica works from a holistic approach that integrates healing, all aspects of self: mind, body, soul, and spirit. A lifelong passion for poetry, nature, music, and an incessant drive for learning nourishes the path of her ever-expanding soul travels.

Jessicajulianlmft@gmail.com

A Woman's Intuition

By Caroline Angel

"If you have light in your heart, you will find your way home."
- Rumi, 13th-Century Poet

It was 5 a.m. on what had been a beautiful June morning, now turning to dawn. I was on foreign soil, thousands of miles away from home. A professional research project had provided an opportunity for my family to accompany me to the beautiful Mediterranean island of Sardinia.

Without warning, my sleep was violently interrupted by the most excruciating, sharp pain in my lower abdomen. It felt like one or both of my ovaries had burst. The pain was profoundly beyond what I had endured birthing three children…combined. Childbirth labor was no match for this pain.

Fever enveloped my body, overheating me. I immediately began sweating profusely. There was no warning. Period. With every breath, it became increasingly more intense. The area where I was sleeping felt like it had turned into a natural hot spring pool. I could hardly take a breath. It was as though someone had sucker-punched me, knocking the wind out of me.

In the midst of this storm, I felt as if I was carrying the ancestral pain or suffering of all women who had come before me. I was exhausted, not only physically, but mentally, emotionally and spiritually too. My body ached as if I had run a marathon for days without being prepared. My light dimmed to the point where I was sure my life force had run out; I thought only about surviving. Each feeling was intense beyond words. Yet, in these moments, my body bore vicarious witness to the combined symptoms of my clients, who had turned to me for help in my practice as an intuitive healer.

Just as quickly as this violent reaction had come on, by 7 a.m. my fever broke. The sweating stopped. I cooled off and the intense pain subsided. Although my bodily functions went back to normal, I couldn't go back to sleep. I was beyond afraid and I didn't know when or if there would be another episode.

After reclaiming my breath and observing that I was still alive, I became aware of what had caused this violent reaction. It was the *bio-identical* hormone cream that had been prescribed for me by a trusted functional medicine doctor.

Through this life-altering experience, I realized how completely out of balance I was. Maybe the Divine Source was sending me a message....

Flashback

I was raised in a culture where being a "good girl" and supporting others was commendable and praised. Through my upbringing, I was valued more for using my mind rather than my heart. My perception—that my heart was not going to help me in this material world—was based upon what I'd been told growing up. My heart wasn't logical, my heart didn't use common sense, my heart didn't always know what was right. My intuition was held in disdain by most of my family members, as well as my husband, who neither valued nor understood it. So, I learned to suffocate it, to turn my back on it; going so far as earning an accounting degree after high school, favoring my logical mind over my heart to solve complicated matters. If I'd paid attention, I would have seen how unhappy my spirit had been for many years; but I didn't listen to the many signs of discontent expressed through my physical symptoms.

A few years ago, like a typical modern woman, I was burning the candle at both ends. Sometimes, I didn't get into bed until 4 a.m. I was taking care of my kids, my husband and my husband's father (who had bladder cancer); my business and my clients; plus, I was volunteering.

Who didn't make the list until 4 a.m.? Me! Although I was only 40 years old, my night sweats were so bad, I'd wake up in the morning with wet sheets, exhausted and without enough energy to get through the day.

I was losing my hair at an alarming rate; I was truly afraid that I'd end up bald in no time! The lack of volume and shine in my hair was noticeable. Going from full-bodied, shiny, healthy hair to thinning hair was a huge hit to my identity, femininity and sensuality. I didn't feel like myself, quite the opposite: unproductive, not being of service and as if I had lost my vibrance. I was exhibiting classic symptoms of hormonal imbalance. And, I felt very alone.

I had such a responsibility for taking care of others that I dismissed my own desires. I was ignorant of the fact that I was abusing my body and therefore taking my whole self for granted. It wasn't until I had this near-death experience that I deeply understood I could not walk this journey alone. I needed the support of my community; one who would help me regain not only myself but my connection to a higher source.

Like many other women, I wanted a quick fix. After running routine tests, a holistic gynecologist prescribed bio-identical hormones. At first, my gut feeling was resistance. However, she pointed out the celebrities and other functional doctors who promoted this "magic" remedy. Even so, honoring my intuition, I asked her to have it compounded in a minute dose. I remember thinking, "If it's in a minute dose, what could go wrong?"

Hindsight is 20/20

Little did I know that by Day 2 of applying this supposedly *benign* quick fix, I would go head to head with my mortality. Even though the episode was violent, sudden and felt like a nightmare, it was a blessing in disguise. The Divine works in unexpected ways. Ultimately, tapping into the imbalanced hormonal experience was a gift that enabled me to empathize deeply and personally, not only in my own life but also in my practice, so that I could be of greater service.

With every shallow breath, the pain and sweating escalated. Curled up in a tiny ball, I was praying that the inhalation I just took was not going to be my last. All I kept thinking of was "I have so much more yet to do and see."

Yes, my intuition guided me back to Source. I realized that all I needed to do was to take care of *myself*. How could I expect to be fully present for my clients, friends and family if I wasn't applying my own gifts, knowledge and expertise to myself *first*?

After getting back on my feet, I noticed a pattern. I became aware of the suffering of other women around me. I saw how modern women are conditioned to being stoic or self-sacrificing in their daily lives. It's my belief that this "martyrdom" neither serves us as women nor the people around us.

What the community of Sardinian women taught me

I have spent the better part of the last 10 years traveling and working with top researchers in the Blue Zones, which are regions of the world with the highest concentration of centenarians, people who live the longest and healthiest, living to over 100 years old. The concept of *blue zones* grew out of the demographic work done by two researchers observing and studying different cultures, diets and lifestyles.

Throughout my own research, I noticed something striking. Unlike the modern woman in many Western cultures who enters menopause with complicated symptoms, the typical centenarian woman eased gently into this beautiful phase of her life.

Interestingly, when asking these centenarian women how they dealt with perimenopause or menopause, their answer was surprising. These women didn't experience any of the symptoms that we modern women experience. They weren't familiar with the symptoms or terms like *hot flashes*. They thought hot flashes meant feeling hot on a hot summer night. They didn't understand that it was like burning from the inside out. My quest was to find out what these women do differently to ease gracefully through perimenopause and menopause. I grew passionately curious. What a serendipitous gift of timing, as I could draw the wisdom from these wise and aging women.

Immersing myself in their world, I went beyond *studying* data about them or trying to confirm an already existing agenda. I developed friendships that transcended time, distance or language barriers. I went on exploration trips with naturalists, who taught me what herbs and foods these centenarian women consumed on a daily basis to maintain balance. For instance, I learned that the many wild herbs the local cows graze upon constitutes the naturally synthetized herbal formula that the women in the village consume to promote balance. These women never needed to consume vitamins, supplements or pharmaceuticals nor use bio-identical hormone replacement therapy, perform lab tests or chase after their health. Because they followed simple natural laws and universal principles, they—unlike modern women—didn't experience severe menopausal symptoms.

Besides healthy lifestyle routines, centenarian women around the world have one of the most important factors of longevity: a strong sense of purpose, spirituality and belonging to a community. It is very typical of these elderly women to engage socially, including dancing, gardening, cooking, praying and gathering.

In Sardinia, where I witnessed the centenarian women's longevity and happiness, I decided to commit, right then and there, to start taking better care of myself and live in my truth. When I returned home, I began studying, reading and interviewing experts in different fields, including endocrinologists, scientists, functional doctors, sleep specialists and more.

I learned that lab tests alone (and, if not done properly) not only didn't give an accurate picture of a woman's state of hormones, it could give a misleading picture resulting in an inaccurate diagnosis and prescription or guidance.

I realized that hormones are a complicated topic—even *amongst* practitioners and the scientific community. We have just scratched the surface. There is more to know beyond what a simple blood test can show.

Just as we each are biochemically individual—which changes from time to time—*women's* hormones continuously change, not only from one decade to another, but from year to year, month to month, week to week and day to day. If lab tests are going to be done, the timing of the test is crucial. There are many variables to consider in getting a good idea about how our hormones are behaving at any given time.

Considering how many moons and stars have to line up to get an accurate diagnosis, it is not surprising that most women who even *seek* help find themselves chasing one doctor and lab test after another. It is expensive, time-consuming, frustrating and deflating; nor does it bring women back into a balanced state.

No wonder women decide to suffer in silence...because our challenges are not addressed properly. Few women have the courage to take matters into their own hands and realize that they have the power to heal from within.

My Learnings

- Technology such as the latest lab tests can be a powerful diagnostic tool to be used in any journey back to health, but their use and interpretation can be fallible.
- Medical doctors in white lab coats are not *always* the experts about our bodies. They don't know our bodies intimately in the same way that we *intuitively* know our own. When it comes to complex topics like hormones, it is wise to surround yourself with a trusted and like-minded community; so, I sought the help of a naturopathic doctor, a sleep specialist, a yoga teacher and an energy healer.
- Over time, I decided to remove myself from toxic relationships. I realized I needed to divorce my husband. I distanced myself from family members, not giving credibility to their opinions about how I should behave. I rebuilt healthy and supportive relationships that are aligned with my life choices.
- Seeing how centenarians go through life gracefully, I learned that having a more conscientious approach to diet and exercise—and, of course, surrounding yourself with the right community—is key. I am grateful for this experience because, through it, I found *my community* and my voice, regained my balance and felt whole once more.

- Over time, my night sweats stopped. I was getting restful sleep. I had more energy during the day. My hair was growing back, full and vibrant. Now that I was taking care of myself first, I found more peace and well-being.

Sometimes we encounter challenges that feel unfair or insurmountable. Seeing these challenges as *opportunities* to break through unhealthy patterns is not always easy. However, surrendering, trusting in the process, letting go and then taking action led by the heart is a practice that yields worthy results. Having a community who sees, values and supports your journey is imperative. May you have the wisdom and discernment to find the community who holds that space for you, to help you become the best version of yourself in this journey called *Life*. I've had good fortune to have found mine.

Caroline Angel is a holistic nutrition and integrative health practitioner who holds certificates in Scientific Foundations of Holistic Nutrition and Completion & Correction Healing’, an energetic healing method.

Founder of *The Whole Transformation and Happy Hormones Program*, Caroline is dedicated to helping women balance their hormones because "every woman deserves to feel vibrant and sexy!"

She is the author of the international best-selling book "Fifty Shades of Grain: The naked truth about eating bread and feeling great" and has spent the better part of a decade traveling and working with top researchers observing and studying centenarians.

www.thewholetransformation.com

THE SPARK OF SURRENDER

By Isolda Restrepo

"Surrender itself is a mighty prayer."

- Sri Ramana Maharishi

What if *community* extends beyond our friends, family, neighbors and locale as we physically know them? What if the source of communing between us and them actually originates as an electric pulse within our own heart and mind? What if, in the act of surrender, a spark ignites that activates an otherwise invisible *tribe of light* who is always standing by, waiting to assist?

Three years ago, I was on death's doorstep. The fact that I am able to sit upright and write this today is primarily the result of the love that I received from my *community*. This loving support came as a direct result of my completely letting go of attachments, ideals, beliefs, judgments, dreams and the life that I knew before.

I let go of what I believed community roles should look like. Some friends and family who I was closest to before my diagnosis are now in the periphery of my life. They didn't know how to show up for a young woman fighting the complex fight of cervical cancer and all that it elicits. Some supported a little from afar; some showed up at first, then fell away when things got hard; some didn't agree with my choices and fell quiet; and one seemingly lost his mind due to the combination of my disease and his own mental illness. This all hurt deeply. It took a while to heal the heartache; but through surrender and grace, I realized that it's nobody's fault; they just didn't know any better. Most of them are still in my life, just a little further out of orbit. One of the many healing roles of a major crisis is cleaning out the old to make way for the new.

Not too long after receiving my diagnosis, I had to sublet my apartment. Fortunately, my aunt—whom I considered as both my second mom and a close friend—lived nearby, so I moved in with her. I had decided from the beginning that I wanted to heal from cancer naturally. I had seen documentaries and read testimonials of people who had, so I figured I could too. I was a very healthy person. I wanted to avoid the toxicity of traditional treatments that would leave me infertile; I had always dreamed of having my own child. Prior to moving in with my aunt, I had tried several protocols. Although I'd never felt better, the menacing mass remained on my cervix.

I intended to continue my natural healing journey. I deeply wanted to be living proof for myself and others that traditional methods weren't the only way to heal. I delved deeply into research. What I didn't know at the time was that this was contrary to what my aunt thought was best for me (and most of my family quietly wanted me to do): traditional chemotherapy and radiation. However, she didn't share this outright. She just welcomed me in with open arms, as I expected family would do in circumstances like these. She appeared to be a source of loving and undying support. I felt safe, loved and inspired to continue my mission of healing myself naturally.

I continued to go to my oncology visits. I saw four different specialists, thinking I might see a variance in treatment approaches. However, until I met my surgeon, they had all said the same thing, with the same austere concern: chemotherapy and radiation.

With surgery, I would still have to sacrifice my fertility (freezing my eggs was sadly too expensive to afford); but it was the least toxic and debilitating of my options. I would no longer be able to *give* life, but I would be able to *keep* my own.

After 8 weeks of healing from surgery, a biopsy showed that the cancer had either come back or hadn't been completely removed; the doctors were uncertain. The next advised treatment was chemotherapy and radiation, about which I was extremely hesitant. Apparently, I had sacrificed my reproductive organs, mourned the death of my lifelong dream of bearing and raising my own child, and yet I STILL had to do the treatments I was trying to avoid.

I continued my research on alternative protocols. I found that the alternative treatment centers with the most credibility were out of the country, far too expensive and therefore out of my reach. I needed some time to digest all of this and research other options for a cure. I had seen too many people get broken-down or die from chemo's (oftentimes irreversible) side effects. What I needed most was time to pray for guidance.

It was at this time of soul-searching that my aunt told me that I needed to leave her home. She wanted me to do chemotherapy and radiation straight away and she could not have me living with her if I wanted to explore alternative healing. My heart sank. I felt the floor fall out from beneath me. All the trust and belief of unconditional love and what family represented to me shattered into a billion pieces. I learned that sometimes family may not actually be there for you when you need them. Sometimes you have to let go, walk away and later find that *community* can show up for you in ways you would never have expected.

I needed respite, so I went to visit my most spiritual friend. Another friend was visiting her from the same Spiritual Psychology program that she was enrolled in. The two of them welcomed me in just as I was, in my current state of mind. They loved and accepted me completely. They nurtured me until I felt whole once again and then invited me to participate in spiritual healing practices that they'd learned in their program. I whole-heartedly agreed. It was divine timing.

I have always believed that illness and healing are multi-faceted. It's not only physical, but psychological, physiological, emotional and spiritual. After all, we are complex, multi-layered beings; why wouldn't our journeys and internal processes be as well? They asked me questions to access the deepest parts of me. They honored my darkest truths. They guided and supported me through forgiveness for others and for myself. They taught me rage therapy, to release resentments and to heal my old wounds. They completely held space for me.

They also introduced me to a Watsu therapist who was one of the most magical healers I have ever met. We absolutely transcended in our sessions together. It was miraculous. It was there that I completely and entirely surrendered. In their warm, non-judgmental, loving arms, I came home. Home to Spirit. Home to myself. If chemotherapy and radiation are how I get through this, so be it. If there is a better way, show me. I completely surrendered.

Meanwhile, another friend of mine showed up, one who had been supportive from the beginning and encouraged my desire for natural healing. He had unlimited funds and offered me a quiet home outside of the city, where I could hole up and focus on healing. This meant I could leave my aunt's home and heal the way I felt was right for me, without judgment, to continue to surrender in peace.

I chose to live in this more spiritual community where there was less pollution and I was surrounded by nature. However, after months of living together, this friend had a psychotic break. Since I knew nothing of his mental history before we became friends, this was shocking to me. He accused me of trying to have him killed, along with many other outlandish things. He was incredibly angry and even sounded like a different person than the one I'd known. He called the sheriff and demanded that I move out, although we were no longer living in the same home. He appeared to have lost his mind and there was no talking sense to him. He was convinced of his dark accusations towards me. At that point, I no longer felt safe.

By now, I had exhausted both my funds and my hand at healing naturally. With repeated surrender, I asked to be shown another way; and, since no recourse had been revealed, I agreed to do traditional therapy. I was halfway through many months of chemotherapy and radiation. I was completely bald, skin and bones, muscles atrophied, in nearly constant agony and hardly able to walk on my own two feet. I was without an income, yet I still needed a place to live. Thankfully, my dear spiritual friend let me stay in her office until I could find a place.

Again, I surrendered. At this point, I had been surrendering often enough to see some evidence of support from a higher source. I remember thinking to myself, "This is absolutely unbelievable. I am a good person and I could never have imagined that anything this crazy could ever have happened to me." I offered my prayer: "I surrender any feeling of victimhood and I am in full trust that there must be a divine plan."

My friends had moved my few possessions out of the house. I was just about to leave when my next-door neighbor came by with groceries and to see how I was doing. I hardly knew this man. I only had introduced myself to him and said "hello" once or twice. I explained what had happened, why I was leaving, and sincerely thanked him for his kindness. He asked if I could spare a little time to go somewhere with him. I was uncertain; however, I trusted his intentions. He drove me to his bank and, incredibly, he gifted me $14,000! He said, "I can only imagine what your medical expenses must be, and the fact that this has happened to you at this time is just absolutely ludicrous." He mentioned that he wanted to give me more, but that was the maximum amount that can be gifted without being taxed. My angel hugged me and wished me well on my journey. I was overwhelmed with emotion.

A week or so later, while I was staying in my friend's office, a family member—who I hadn't heard from or spoken with since I was maybe five years old—unexpectedly checked in on me. He had learned of my recent health challenge on Facebook. I surrendered my pride and told him of the stressful and fragile state in which I found myself. He, by the grace of God (I never thought I would say such a thing, let alone to feel it coruscate through my entire being), simply told me not to worry. "Find a peaceful and safe place to live and I will take care of it. Healing is the most important thing right now," he said. I had no idea how humongous his heart was nor that he had the means to support me in such a way. Without question, I was in desperate need, without any idea of how I would get through this ordeal. As I continued to trust and surrender, his angelic contribution was further evidence of how I was being divinely held.

While the sparks of healing light came in and out during my journey, of varying proximity and brightness, I'd be remiss not to mention one light; the brightest, most constant and steady light in my community: my little sister. Despite other family members falling off the radar or not coming in until later in my journey, my younger sister was there for me from the very beginning, until the very end, every step of the way.

She stood up for me in the face of my family, who just couldn't understand my choices, when I wasn't there to explain or defend myself. She never needed me to explain. She implicitly understood me and stood steadfast. My sister effortlessly showed up in the way that I thought family *should*. She was the only person in my family who validated and supported me after my aunt closed her door to me. She used her sick and vacation days to fly across the country to hold my hand and sit with me through varying times of anguish. My sister shaved her head when I lost my hair, so that I didn't have to bear that vulnerability on my own. She also gave me my dog, Dexter, who was an extension of her and was with me when she couldn't be. Through the darkest, scariest, most painful and unbearable times of uncertainty and terror, Dexter uplifted and made me laugh; gave me smiles, cuddles, and a reason to get out and walk, even if just twice briefly each day, despite my pain and sadness.

Later, through a distant friend of my sister's, I met my somatic therapist, who played a major role in remediating my decimated, brittle and painful pelvic tissues after all the radiation.

I have no idea what it was like for her to have her big sister whittled down to such frailty and emaciation before her eyes. To witness the one who she often looked up to barely hanging onto life as we knew it could not have been easy. But she never broke down in front of me, not once. She never showed one iota of weakness or doubt. She stood taller and shone brighter than any guiding light ever has. Her unflagging conviction that I would get through it all made me believe that I would. Her unparalleled strength and loving support kept my light shining. She was my most brilliant shining light—my North Star.

My older sister was an incredible beacon of loving and uplifting light as well. She also shaved part of her head with us in solidarity, which ended up being quite fitting for her as the badass Canadian songbird rock star that she is! She also took time off from work to come down from Canada to sit with me, to laugh with me, to cook for me and to hold me. In full transparency, as much as I loved her dearly, I did not feel the same unwavering understanding and steadfastness that I did with my younger sister during this dark time of need. Though it hurt deeply, I decided to let that go, and to believe that we don't have to see things exactly eye to eye for me to have felt held and seen by her. I knew that she was genuinely giving me the most and very best support that she could at the time.

One of the sweetest memories I have from that time was of her singing "Candle on the Water" to me, both on the phone and in person. This song is from *Pete's Dragon*, one of our beloved animated childhood favorites. I hadn't even thought of it since I was a young girl. The sweet, angelic sound of my sister's soft yet soul-stirring voice singing this nostalgic melody brought a depth of tears to my eyes and a kindling warmth to my heart that nothing nor no one else ever could have.

"I'll be your candle on the water
This flame inside of me will grow
Keep holding on, you'll make it
Here's my hand, so take it
Look for me reaching out to show
As sure as rivers flow
I'll never let you go.
I'll never let you go…"

I will never forget the people who came forward during my time of need. These people touched my heart deeply and profoundly. My fight was both taxing and overwhelming. The world around me felt dark, uncertain and alien…and so did I. I was no longer in the body and mind that I once knew, and I couldn't enjoy life the way I used to. I was in too much pain, could hardly eat and was depressed a lot of the time. My light was very close to burning out. After a certain point, all I could do was surrender into the experience.

Whenever I felt like giving up, someone from my loving community stepped in. Each time they did it felt like nudges from the divine telling me to hold on. Every time I received kindness, a hug, words of encouragement or a gift, it added fuel to my flame. As my light grew stronger and brighter, I inspired others in my community by showing resilience. When others told me that I was an inspiration to them, it amplified my light even more.

The kindness of these people who formed my community, gave me faith—faith in humanity, faith in strangers, and faith in the divine. These experiences made me want to stay in the fight and to keep living when oftentimes I didn't know if it was worth it. I now see with a new set of eyes, hear with a new set of ears and feel with an expanded and immeasurably more compassionate heart. I am so hungry to extend this burning light of loving support to anyone who may need it as I continue on my path. I will always keep this fire burning and can hardly wait to help the next person who may need it.

I believe that if we are experiencing hardship, have a genuine desire to move and to grow through it and to come out the other side as a *victor* rather than as a victim, the possibilities of expansion and grace are inevitable and vast. I believe that the further we go inward, ask for help, listen and *completely surrender,* we will be met with an equal measure of guiding light. This light may take the form of an idea or a moment of realization, a new opportunity presenting itself, or it may take the form of another person. If we truly let go and surrender control, unforeseen possibilities are there waiting for us and they are endless.

In surrendering into the void, fully, completely and with absolute trust, I let go of the familiar path, which as it crumbled beneath me made way for a divine yellow brick road paved with the most lovable, supportive and magical characters: A *community* of love and light who helped to lead me back home…to myself.

Isolda Restrepo is a writer, intuitive empath, and lightworker who continues to create, heal, and be of service as she seeks her next adventure.

Finding the True Me

By Barbara Savin

"The best way to find yourself is to lose yourself in the service of others."
- Mahatma Gandhi

I was born into a typical first-generation American family—loving and traditional—in Coney Island, New York, during those idyllic, postwar days of the early baby boom. I felt secure and protected by my parents, Sophia and Frank. I learned my values from my adoring grandparents; Isidore, a tailor, and Samuel, a postal worker, both hardworking and striving for a better future. Grandma Rose, from Russia, was always giving of herself through volunteering and Grandma Jenny, from Istanbul, was a *healer*.

This is where my classic mid-century tale takes a fork in the road. You see, energy healing has always been a formative part of my life. As children, my sister and I believed our Grandma Jenny had magical powers! Since she regularly performed healing work on us, we rarely got sick. We would beg her to *stop* healing us so we could get sick and stay home from school like the other kids. Naturally, she never paid attention to our childish requests and continued to heal and clear her darling granddaughters.

I soon realized that I *too* was magical like Grandma Jenny. Even as a child, I knew I had the same gifts. I was able to hear, feel, and sense spirits; I was never alone. I had many spirit *friends* with whom only I could see and speak to. Deceased relatives such as Grandma Jenny's son John (he died in WWII) and her sister, Great-Aunt Bella, would show up as well as cats and other animals and angelic beings. My mother said it was my imagination and didn't acknowledge it, while my grandmother cautioned me to keep it under wraps. Therefore, I kept silent about my secret in public for many years.

It was risky for me, but sometimes—like a reluctant superhero—I had to unmask and reveal my abilities at school. If I sensed a friend was about to get hurt on the playground, I'd have to warn them *not* to do that thing. Inevitably, they didn't listen, would get hurt and blame me; I was bullied a lot in retribution. Universally, kids want to belong. Being weird was definitely not a good way to stand out.

I could see why Grandma Jenny would *shush* me protectively, her Turkish accent strong yet endearing: "Less is best...don't say anything...they'll put *us* away in a crazy hospital!" She realized that I had intuitive abilities and was able to feel people's energies. Remember, this was the 1950s-early 1960s, when society wasn't yet as open about or receptive to the paranormal as we are currently. There were still traces of the mindset that healers and intuitive individuals were witches or somehow unholy.

When I was 12, I had a near-death experience. A serious freak accident had impaled a fence post into my stomach. I'll spare you the gory details, but Grandma Jenny did her healing work on me in the hospital; eventually, remarkably, I had a full recovery. From then on, Grandma Jenny knew with certainty how much my body and soul wanted to allow my passion and purpose to come forward, but she still was determined to protect me. So, as she was clearing me, she'd tell me to trust in God's healing and showed me how to protect my energy.

Meanwhile, Grandma Rose's exemplary behavior taught me that the greatest gift you can give is the gift of yourself to someone in need. During our frequent visits to her apartment, my sister and I would find her in a flurry of activity as she busily prepared food or other things to bring to needy people, volunteer at the Red Cross or wherever else she was needed. At first, I didn't quite grasp that lesson because, from my child's perspective, we didn't have much. Weren't *we* needy? Why did *I* have to give away things when *I* needed clothes? However, whatever Grandma Rose asked us to do, we did without question because we loved being with her and often accompanied her on many occasions as her little volunteers.

Fast-forward to May 1966, just days away from my graduation from Lafayette High School in Brooklyn, a day I'd been looking forward to for years. I was going to graduate with honors and receive the Mayor's Award. I pictured Grandma Jenny and Grandma Rose sitting together in the audience, their faces beaming with pride as my name was called to receive this award....

The phone rang shrilly at two o'clock in the morning, interrupting my dream with the worst news of my 18 years: Grandma Jenny had died. She was only sixty-four. She was supposed to celebrate my most important day with me...and now she was gone. She was such a huge influence in my life. I was devastated. I was hurt. I was angry. How could she do this to me? I was ashamed of my thought. Instead, I blamed God: How could God take someone who loved me so deeply? My adolescent anger had far-reaching consequences....

I was so angry with God—that my grandmother wouldn't be there to witness my highest achievement—that, right then and there, I decided to stop doing healings; not even for my closest friends, the ones who had never made fun of my ability. When they'd ask, I'd tell them flatly: "I'm sorry, but I don't believe in God's healing anymore." When I saw spirits or heard a voiceless voice, I would say, "You're not real; go away and stop speaking to me. Leave me alone." This, I thought, was my way of *punishing* God for taking Grandma Jenny. She always said, "Only God does healing." So, I associated *not* doing healing with punishing God.

I'm going to share something now that I've never told anyone. Not even my mother. A secret I've held onto for 20 years. Two weeks before my graduation, I dreamed that Grandma Jenny had died and we buried her in a white dress. So, you see, I thought I had killed her. My guilt, on top of my grief and my disappointment rendered me inconsolable and unable to forgive myself.

Back then, we lived on the second floor of the projects. About two weeks after she died, in the foyer, a cloud of white fog emanated and I could make out the vague figure of my Grandma Jenny. I was in total disbelieve to see her spirit in my foyer. But she called out to me soothingly in her familiar voice with my pet name: "*Barbaracita*, don't be afraid. Don't be so angry." She looked exactly the same as she had in my dream—wearing that white dress! I was comforted. Many years later, I approached my mother with curiosity: "Mom, what was Grandma Jenny wearing when you buried her?" My mother's quick response gave me chills: "She wanted to be buried in her wedding dress…."

In the long run, though, punishing myself, my grandmother and God—and denying my truth—boomeranged. As the years went on, *my* body began to break down with chronic migraines and fatigue. I was constantly sick, always stressed, working at a job I disliked *while* raising two children. It wasn't until years later that I had the maturity and the spiritual perspective to realize that Grandma Jenny's soul had needed to leave then. I forgave her; I forgave myself, and I got back to believing in God, beginning my true healing.

A decade or so after I'd denounced healing work, my niece Stefanie saw a flyer for a Reiki healing circle in Staten Island. Neither of us knew about Reiki; but since we were both in poor shape physically and emotionally, we decided to check it out. The practitioners performed Reiki on us, basically a laying of hands to produce a beneficial effect by balancing the body's energy fields. I immediately recognized this sensation from Grandma Jenny's healings! I was moved to tears from the comfort of her blessed memory. In that moment, I realigned with God's healing energy and could no longer deny that this was my nature. I clearly saw that my path was healing—first myself and then others.

Now in my 40s, for the first time since Grandma Jenny's death, I understood that healing myself needed to come from *within*. I focused on doing self-healings at least twice a day for a month. I noticed not only improvements in my health but also insights and self-awareness. I realized I both hated and loved parts of myself; it was a spiritual paradox. The agenda was to embrace what I feared, forgive Grandma Jenny for dying and get back to God. Perhaps the most important lesson was learning to love myself for who I was at my core: a healer.

Giving myself healing treatments made me realize the pain I was experiencing was not only physical but also rooted in emotional and spiritual challenges. When a miracle happened, it was powerful evidence of a higher presence.

At the time, I was experiencing black particles floating in front of my eyes (floaters), making it hard to see. While looking in the mirror and speaking to myself, I implored God for assistance. I begged God to help me understand what was happening and to please remove the black particles. Suddenly, I heard a voice within me say, "All you need to do is ask." Immediately, the black particles disappeared. In that very moment, I realized God does listen and speak to us, but we often choose not to hear. God sees and understands us, but we often choose not to see nor understand ourselves. God loves us unconditionally, but we choose to love conditionally. Once I truly began believing in God again, miracles continued to happen. My body became pain-free and chronic fatigue a thing of the past. No more headaches, no more pain; I felt functionally human again, filled with love and happiness.

At that point, I committed to deepening my knowledge of healing. I studied Pranic healing and hypnotherapy; I became a hypnotherapist and meditation instructor; I learned Healing Touch and became a Reiki Master/Teacher. Whenever I offered someone a healing session, I experienced a sense of complete peacefulness. My inner being felt centered and balanced, filled with God's light the way I used to feel with Grandma Jenny's healings. There was no doubt that I was finally aligning with my passion and purpose.

Then my trust and faith in God, along with my healing abilities were truly put to the test on **September 11, 2001....**

The day began as usual. My husband woke up early and had to be at work in Manhattan at 7 a.m. He kissed me goodbye, left the house, drove to the Staten Island Ferry and boarded the 6:20 a.m. boat to the southern tip of Manhattan. From there, he'd take the IRT train to the World Trade Center station, walk up the stairs to the concourse of the North Tower. At 8:30 a.m., he'd break for breakfast and meet our son. Together, they'd go to the Towers for breakfast. Normal....

My husband worked for Bell Atlantic (now Verizon) at 140 West Street; my son worked for Ladenburg Financial Services in the Century

Building on Church Street. Both buildings were across the street from the World Trade Center. I was getting ready to go to work at Island Women's Medical, where I helped clients with Reiki, when I received a call from one of my husband's coworkers asking if he'd gone to work. "Of course, he did," I answered. I'd seen him leave the house. "He's probably at the World Trade Center having breakfast with our son."

You know what happened next…but I still was unaware, my world still intact. However, as she uttered the next words, my blood turned to ice: "You don't know what happened?" "Noooo…" I held my breath. "A plane flew into the Twin Towers…." I hung up before she finished the sentence and immediately turned on the television. I figured (hoped, prayed) that maybe it was a *small* plane that had hit the World Trade Center; but, boy, was I ever wrong. As the enormity of the disaster hit me full force, I began shaking uncontrollably, overcome with anxiety and panic. I feared the worst…and it got worse moments later when the second plane hit the building and the first tower collapsed.

Repeatedly, frantically, I tried calling my husband and son; but the phones weren't working. I just heard busy signals. I screamed in fear and frustration and railed against God once again: "What is happening, God?" Busy signals. I fell to my bedroom floor in tears not knowing what to do. I couldn't think or function; I almost couldn't breathe. Sensing my distress, my sweet Rottweiler, Sammy, came over and laid his head on my leg. Sammy was my "Reiki Master" dog, always a source of comfort and healing not just to me but to others. After sobbing hysterically for quite a while, I heard an inner voice: "Calm yourself, Barbara; do your healing. *Trust* that everything will be fine." I knew the situation was completely out of my control. I asked God for his healing energy and gently put my hands on my heart. I needed to calm down because it felt like I was having a heart attack. I was numb, in a state of sheer panic. I prayed, not just for my two, but for everyone as I stayed glued to the television in horror. I could see the damage to the buildings where my son and husband worked.

As the morning ticked by in excruciating minutes, I was able to receive calls but still could not reach my husband nor my son. Our daughter in California called, frantically asking me if I'd heard from them. Sadly, I had no news to offer her, hoping that no news was good news. My parents, my sister in Florida, friends from other states, all calling hoping for the best but fearing the worst.

Shortly after noon, God must have heard my prayers, because my son's ex-wife called at 12:30 with a message. Luckily, she had stayed home from work that day, so she hadn't gone into Manhattan. She'd been able to get through to my husband on her AT&T service. My husband gave her the uptown address of where he was heading if and when she heard from our son. Nearly four frantic hours later, at 4:00 p.m., he called. "Hold on," he said, "someone wants to talk to you." It was my son. Grateful beyond words, I sobbed into the phone.

Ultimately, along with many others, they were able to get on a train that went underground to Brooklyn and then take a bus that would bring them home. Boarding it at 8:00 p.m., they had no idea when it would get to Staten Island. It was hard to see through my tears and the darkness as I drove to the commuter parking lot an hour later, prepared to wait as long as it took until I could hug them both again. I didn't think I'd ever let go…. When I pulled up, I was struck by the sheer number of people crowded together, all waiting for their loved ones. I remember getting out of my car and being embraced by people I didn't even know—strangers really—bonded by shock as well as bittersweet relief that ours were the lucky ones who were coming home. We, the emotional survivors, hugged and cried, sharing the hours until well past midnight when the bus finally arrived. They stepped off the bus at 1 a.m., weary, worn out, sad and depressed. I ran to them, sobbing. No words were needed; our tears spoke volumes. Safe at home, I thanked God for watching over them, but prayed, sadly, for the ones who hadn't made it.

I was beyond grateful, so I turned my energy to helping the community. I volunteered for hospice care at hospitals, helping HIV, AIDS and cancer patients. For me, though, the deepest honor was being called upon to be one of the few to help out with healing and meditation at the community tents put up by The Salvation Army and Red Cross near the Staten Island ferry. These special tents were for the First Responders, the FBI, the workers and the like, who were involved in the 9/11 recovery and rescue. I *needed* to do it for myself as well as for them; we all needed healing. Nearby was where they brought pieces of the buildings and salvaged personal items such as pictures and jewelry. It was extremely emotional to see those public and intimate items, symbolic of such devastating loss.

Across the street from the Towers, 350 teenage girls at St. Peter's Catholic High School witnessed the first plane hitting the tower. I was asked to lead a meditation for them to help clear their trauma and begin their healing, so they might start to feel safe again after 9/11. This was the first of many facilities at which I eagerly volunteered. It was clear to me that my purpose was to be there to help those First Responders and others who were suffering in silence from 9/11 and its fallout. In the face of this incomprehensible disaster, many had to hold back their emotions in order to function. I felt this whole experience deeply, a profound reminder of the world outside of myself and how I, as a healer, fit into it. Giving back to those who needed healing helped me shift the focus away from my personal challenges to the real-life struggles and immediate needs of others. I remember feeling that my soul was overwhelmed with light during this dark time; I wanted to share that light with everyone, to be there for them. I believe that the impact we have on others intensifies when we become part of something bigger than ourselves. The First Responders—everyone really—were so grateful for my help; I simply offered them hands-on healing, just listened or whatever else was needed. By bearing silent witness with compassion, in return, their gift to me was my spiritual growth.

I finally grasped the full sense of what my Grandma Rose had meant when she said to *give of yourself unconditionally*, especially when you are grateful for everything you have. I was beyond grateful on 9/11 and in the days following. As I reflect back on my life, my world completely changed when I volunteered. The more I gave of myself to others, the more my self-confidence, self-esteem and feelings of self-worth in my abilities grew. The volunteering allowed me the chance to break out of my daily routine, and allowed me to see and experience the many challenges that actually broadened my skills as an energy healer and hypnotherapist. In my heart, I was providing hope to those that needed it including myself. Volunteering for my community was a win-win: true healing and giving unconditionally of myself. I profoundly understood what my purpose in life was through giving service to others. That message rang out extremely loud and clear once I tuned into that vibration. The key was unmistakable: it simply felt natural to give back. I know without a doubt that there is a greater power guiding and showing me the way to share that divine light within me.

By 2004, we felt it was time to leave the East Coast and moved to California to be with our grandchildren, our family community. Shortly thereafter, I heard about a job opportunity at the landmark California Health & Longevity Institute that was about to open at The Four Seasons Hotel in Westlake Village. Over 100 people applied for the position of energy healing specialist and clinical hypnotherapist. God surely must have believed in me and pushed my name to the top of that list because I was the one chosen. I'm sure that all those hours of healing work and volunteering during one of the worst contemporary U.S. disasters stood out as an impressive credential during my extensive interview with the Director.

I also was fortunate to have worked with a renowned medical doctor, a functional medicine specialist and author, at her local holistic wellness center. I worked at both facilities for over 11 years, until I decided it was time to open my own center.

Looking back over my 30 years as an energy healing practitioner in East and West Coast communities, I've worked with thousands of clients suffering from a myriad of physical, emotional, mental and spiritual issues. It still is wonderful, miraculous "work," and I am so blessed to be able to be of service.

Today, I am grateful for all of my life experiences. I commit to acknowledging the blessings in each moment and to remain humble. Life is an incredible journey and dreams do come true as long as you have faith and community.

Barbara E. Savin is the author of *Gentle Energy Touch: The Beginner's Guide to Hands-on Healing* and the radio host of *Motivate Your Life* on healthylife.net. She's a licensed Reiki Master Teacher, energy healing specialist, clinical hypnotherapist, life coach, and inspirational speaker. Barbara believes you can create anything you set your mind to do and shares her passion for transformation by teaching energy healing and leading meditation and healing circles and gratitude and appreciation workshops.

www.MotivateYourLife.Net

Rooted in Faith

By Mira Rocca

"A life without community is not how G-d intended for us to live!"
- Anonymous

I was born in Vilnius, Lithuania. A land that once was home to a very soulful Jewish community. A space where practicing Judaism was not only accepted but celebrated. As Word War II and the Holocaust fell upon the land and its people, practicing Judaism was no longer safe, no longer sacred. Both my maternal and paternal grandparents were involved in WWII: either fighting in the Russian Army or as victims of the Holocaust.

The postwar remnants of hate and intolerance for Jews was frightening. Living under Communist rule restricted our ability to experience religious and personal freedom. My family fled Lithuania when I was almost three, eleven years before the fall of the USSR. My parents saw the writing on the wall; they foresaw the lack of opportunity for my brother and me, and that became their driving force to leave the country. They were uncomfortable—terrified really—to practice our religion, and that was unacceptable. Fear was in charge; it was real, and it justified the need to escape. And it stayed that way for quite some time.

When we became American citizens, we changed our last name from Epshteyn to Epstein, so as not to stand out as being "too Russian." There was such desperation to fit in, to assimilate; but, more important, was to feel safe. At that point, it wasn't clear to me what *wasn't* safe:

being Russian or being Jewish. Regardless, my mind combined the two labels and they became a part of my life story that I wanted to cover up.

We were fearful, we were brave, and we were stuck in survival mode for a very long time…maybe my parents still are. I was so accustomed to lugging around the baggage packed with my family's ancestral trauma, I didn't know how heavy it was…until I put it down long enough to unravel our history and come to terms with it; ultimately, to accept and honor it and write a new chapter with a happier ending. Survival mode was my uncomfortable default. I didn't realize that there was an alternative until I began freely speaking my truth aloud about being Jewish, strengthening this layer of my foundation, allowing myself to stand with G-d in my truth.

Don't get me wrong; my parents made a nice life for us in the United States. I grew up in suburban Los Angeles. I went to Hebrew school. I went to synagogue for the High Holy Days. I had a Bat Mitzvah. Everything felt "normal." But it wasn't until I truly experienced *freedom*, that I realized how suppressed I actually was.

My first taste of freedom began in Australia. At thirteen, we moved there for two years for a job opportunity that my mother could not pass up. This was where I planted my first seed of safety. Riding the trolley home from school, I remember a new friend asking me if I was Jewish and I stammered out: "I'm Russian." That label felt less threatening to voice out loud. And the sky didn't fall. I noticed how speaking my truth made me feel calmer. The conversation continued. "OK, so you're Russian…but are you Jewish?" she pressed. "Because *I am both*," she proclaimed. I was dumbfounded and just stared at her for what felt like a whole lifetime while my paradigm shifted. She was my first friend in Australia, my first seedling of safety in origin, in religion and, as I would soon discover—in *community*!

During those two years in Australia, I found love and comfort in being Russian AND being Jewish. The parameter that changed was finding my community and how that brought me closer to G-d. Being around other Russian Jews who *loved and embraced* the same foundation as mine created that safe space I craved. Being around people who not only acknowledged their history, but *celebrated* it, made room for me to do the same and I loved that. The more I loved, the less I feared. The more I loved, the prouder I was. The more I opened my heart, the more I felt a soul connection. The more I loved, the louder my voice grew in speaking my truth that I Am the *And*.

As I began to feel more comfortable with my identity, I felt connected to my new community as well. I danced a dance of joy and belonging. I finally felt like I was part of something bigger than myself and that it was safe to be the fully integrated Me.

I noticed new places where my soul felt that sense of familiarity. When I visited Israel for the first time, I cried tears of relief; my soul felt like it had come *home*. Or when I'd sit teary-eyed in the *sanctuary* of my daughter's Jewish preschool, enjoying that word in its fullest meaning. Simultaneously knowing and remembering feeling *home*, with permission to be my *whole* self within a community. Each time I hear my children speak about how proud they are to be Jewish, my heart swells and my pride strengthens.

As with anything in life, there is a balance. A cause and effect. A yin and a yang. Two experiences happening at the same time. Duality. I feel so proud, yet so confused by the current hate that weaves its way through our world, through my community. I feel so proud to be Jewish and someone spray paints swastikas on the temple preschool. Haven't we evolved past that? It's been 40 years since my family fled our homeland for religious freedom.

Humans collectively evolve, spiraling upwards in consciousness, reliving similar pieces of our history, yet with a new sense of awareness supported by our cohesive community, encouraging a bolder, more confident ability to speak up even louder. Within my community, I feel a renewed faith—call it surrender; I feel G-d is by my side and I know I can handle more and still thrive.

Whenever there is a shooting here in the United States or an anti-Semitic attack at a temple anywhere in the world, I find myself wanting to flee back to Australia. Australia is symbolic of that safe place and sense of belonging to a tribe. Now I realize that Australia itself is not my *safe* place: it's what that community awakened *within* me, that is. Australia allowed me to thrive within the vulnerability of my religion.

It's like having a string of not-so-amazing boyfriends, and then one comes along and awakens that feeling of being loved. We cling to that ONE, thinking he's the *only* one ever who can make us feel special. And, to feel that wholeness again, we must remain with him. But the truth is, when we feel the absence of him, it awakens that desire for wholeness that lies dormant *within* us. I know that both safety and vulnerability lie within me and it's my relationship with G-d that makes me whole.

Healing and safety and community are an interchangeable dance. I will look back on the hate and intolerance just long enough to allow my core beliefs to shine through even more brightly, not only within my sacred community, but within all aspects of my life. For every example that I can access from my history about feeling separation as a Jew, I now have story upon story to support my more solid and secure foundation within my Judaic community. At the soul level, where it's incontrovertible, I know a deep sense of belonging and pride.

I evolve and grow, and my sense of community and belonging shift along with it. Embracing my identity within the Jewish tradition, I feel my spirituality begin to weave within that and form an even stronger foundation. I used to believe that spirituality and religion were separate. Now, I'm more comfortable blending the spiritual into the religious core. While a single tree has many roots and branches, they are all part of the whole. As the roots of my tree began healing, it allows my own branches to thrive; and like a tree, my connection to my community deepens. To have someone witness my story, my experience, and love and accept me feels like pure magic to my soul. A healing exhale. This layer to my foundation is solid.

I am the mother of two daughters and a son. As my girls begin to hit the sweet spot of awakening into womanhood and soul-shifting, I feel empowered to hold space for them, to welcome them into a community of women and sacredness in which they too can feel safe and grow and evolve…and belong. I have reread The Red Tent and Rebecca Campbell's Rise Sister Rise. I read Deborah Feldman's Unorthodox and her follow-up book, The Exodus. Untamed by Glennon Doyle and Brené Brown's Braving the Wilderness round out this bibliography I've drawn upon to satisfy my craving for an even deeper sense of belonging within a smaller circle, because I believe there is magic and wisdom and grace and strength when women gather vulnerably in a circle. Knowing that in our small community all of my children matter and that they are loved. I'm looking forward with excitement to see what they will choose to build upon that foundation.

Isolated at home during this massive Corona virus "pause" button is triggering my deepest desire—*to belong* to a tribe—to resurface. The devastation of COVID-19 and the resulting unprecedented government-ordered quarantine has shut down the temples and places of worship indefinitely, precisely at a challenging time when we most need the reassurance of our faith and community.

What's different for me now is that I'm dusting off my intuition, trusting my inner voice, and allowing my soul to speak up in this historic yet deeply personal moment. I'm hearing a new story, not of separation, but of holistic integration with my life lessons. While it seems that the external environment has been shut down, and it's easy to fall prey to a feeling of scarcity, I know that I have more than enough reserves within me, with G-d. The trauma of believing I ever was separate is evaporating in the mist of ancestral time. I am now and always will be a community of One connected to All.

Mira Rocca is an Integrative Psychotherapist and Wellness Coach. She is also Horse-Inspired Growth and Healing (HIGH) certified at Big Heart Ranch in Malibu, a nature-based community wellness center and animal rescue sanctuary where people and animals inspire each other. Mira is a happily married, busy mother of three who lives and works in beautiful Calabasas, California.

www.mirarocca.com

INFINITE WISDOM FROM OUR OCEAN FAMILY

By Heather Green

"The ocean stirs the heart, inspires the imagination and brings eternal joy to the soul."

- Robert Wyland, Artist and Conservationist

I'll never forget the day I first arrived at the beach near my new place. Two lonely years after my divorce, I was further burdened by the heartbreak of the passing of my two oldest horses and had anxiety over an uncertain financial and career situation. I decided to move to Monterey on a whim. I was more than happy to leave behind my old life in a city where I was often isolated from close friends and any real sense of community. But I knew I was meant to be here when unexpectedly I was offered a studio apartment just five minutes walking distance to Monterey Bay and Del Monte Beach. I've always shared a special connection with the ocean, so I was overjoyed! Yet, I definitely had some doubts.

I wondered what was next for me here. I had no plan. And working as a professional psychic and healer from a different location could mean losing some of my former clientele, especially those who prefer in-person sessions. Still, I trusted the feeling of lightness and expansion that came through with my intuitive direction to make this move. So, as I sat on the beach that day, I stared at the water and started to relax. The rhythmic waves soothed and mesmerized me. And then I heard a voice in my mind. It said, "We can help each other."

Intuitively, I knew it was coming from the water. It felt as though the ocean and all sea life were speaking to me as one big community or collective. Immediately, I saw an image of myself writing notes in a small notebook. I was upstairs in an important building and needed to get the memos to the right people in a hurry. This institution or organization was concerned with the welfare of the dolphins and whales.

In the next moment, the scene shifted back to the water. I knew the whales were connecting with me energetically, even though I could not see them with my physical eyes. Their voices resounded inside of me: "The darkness is coming for us." Through my body, I could sense ominous interfering energies that included sound waves and other loud noises in and around the water. I was already well aware that a variety of environmental toxins were affecting the food supply and health of the cetaceans and other sea life on the West Coast of the U.S. But more than anything, I hoped that no one would purposely set out to harm these magnificent beings.

As far back as I can remember, I have always sensed that highly evolved souls were incarnated in many of these intelligent dolphin and whale beings. I know their communication, songs, and the routes and patterns they travel in the sea are not only a way of going about their natural lives. At times, this is also how and when they radiate energy that can heal particular areas of the sea and the earth. Humans benefit from this as well. When we are at the beach, on a boat or near the sea, we can receive these higher frequencies that transform us on a body, mind and spirit level.

Those spring days of 2019 passed slowly as I got acquainted with my new city. When I wasn't working with private clients over the phone, I spent much of my free time meditating to help me stay calm and confident in the midst of the unknown. One day, as I emerged from this deeply peaceful state, I saw my landlady's cat perched on the fence outside my window, framed by an expansive view of the ocean behind him. Through my psychic vision, I saw a large golden chalice balancing in the air in front of the cat. Sparkling coins, beautiful colors and flowers overflowed from the cup. It reminded me of how abundance can show up in many forms. As I had this thought, I felt the ocean beckoning. I knew it was important that I make physical contact with her.

From that day on, I regularly took barefoot beach strolls, letting the waves wash over my feet, and splashing my legs. Within a couple of months, I was feeling uplifted, energized and optimistic about the future. I was even more blessed after my neighbor loaned me her wetsuit early that summer. On especially warm days, when the wind and sea were calm, I went swimming. While in this deep communion with the water, I experienced more laughter, joy and peace than I had in years. I felt completely free, knowing all was well and exactly how it should be.

The abundance of greater emotional well-being, health and vitality that came into my life through my deepening connection and routine visits with the ocean collective spread to other life areas. I was grateful to live and flourish in a place with so much beauty. The gorgeous sand dunes, ocean waves and diverse flower gardens that I woke up to every day took my breath away. On top of this, I was getting offers to serve within my community. I began doing readings by request for people and their animals at two book and gift shops in the area.

Late that spring and early summer, I started to read about the ocean collective on social media and learn more about her environment from a lecture I attended locally. I knew that humanity's desire to meet the needs of wild animals and the earth was necessary if we wanted to live in a thriving world. There are many researchers and welfare groups that educate about how pollution and sound disturbances, such as increased ocean traffic and sonar devices, can negatively impact sea life. Having lived in Morro Bay and Monterey, I also have heard from community members about dolphins and whales getting stuck or injured in outdated or defective fishing nets meant to catch smaller fish. I couldn't imagine going back to a time where whaling was a reality; but in September 2019, I learned that it was happening again in Japan.

Despite these known environmental hardships, I focused on getting out healing and enlightening messages that the ocean collective had shared with me to help our human community. This would also emphasize the importance that the ocean and sea life have on our physical and spiritual evolution. In return, this could benefit the ocean collective, as more humans are inspired to care for her well-being. I started sharing the ocean collective's messages on Facebook, at a couple of in-person and online events and at two local gatherings that summer and fall.

After a refreshing swim and taking time to rest in the sun on the beach, a powerful message came to me from the whale collective. I heard them begin: "A new dawn is coming...one of freedom, strength and knowing. We weave the golden strands of light throughout your oceans, bringing a lightness into your world and to those who are ready to release the burdens they carry and be in peace. The time of awakening is here. There can be no going back. Be gentle with your newborn baby selves, as you see the world through eyes of wonder and innocence. Those who recognize this newfound freedom are the leaders on the pathway of peace."

Again, in late January 2020, they spoke to me abruptly as I finished a long walk on the beach. This message foreshadowed the COVID-19 pandemic that was soon to affect the U.S. "We are entering a new era... one of love and joy and promise. This is a time period of balance and sustenance, with more becoming available for all. The power of love so prevalent in your world and selves is shaking things up—working behind the scenes and altering our shared realities. No obstacle is ever insurmountable while in the face of this force. Stay steady on your path and course but be ready to change direction at a moment's notice if guided to do so. Everything you could ever need or desire can be found inside of you. The wait is over; be who you came here to be and set yourselves free."

Over the spring and summer of 2020, I've felt the steadfast support of the ocean collective in my healing and growth process. But one mystical encounter stands out in my mind and heart. Resting on my favorite spot at my beach, I asked her if she could help me let go of the remaining emotions still connecting me with my old life. When I felt the affirmative inside, I took a deep breath and released lingering anxiety about my future work and finances. I began to give up the guilt over past mistakes. I let go of the hurt, fear and mistrust related to relationships that didn't work out. As it all lifted out of me, I felt the ocean collective's energy reach out and pull in these emotions, seemingly transforming them into something beneficial as they disappeared into her dark depths.

As I finished the healing, in my mind's eye, I saw a stack of books fastened by a belt, floating towards the water. Was this my old learning, karma or conditioning being released? I couldn't be sure. Then I saw the flash of sparklers, a magnet and a man who was connected to the sea in some way. He either surfed, owned a boat or was called to serve on behalf of the ocean collective—perhaps all of the above!

I didn't know if or how any of this would unfold in my life, but I was sure it would be interesting to find out. Maybe I was in for an adventure that would spark my excitement and possibly draw to me an important connection or a new career partnership? In the meantime, I could only be patient.

As the summer days of 2020 passed by, a new online work opportunity came in that could allow me to expand my clientele. My heart was full of appreciation for all the new friendships and connections I had made over the last year since moving to Monterey. Yet there was another doubt that still burdened me. I needed to feel safe being seen and practicing on a bigger scale as an intuitive and channel. I knew this required me to be vulnerable. I needed to deeply trust in myself and my true destiny.

After a recent swim on a cool day in July, the ocean collective delivered a sudden message that set me at ease. She said, "Wipe the past away like a clean slate. You are free. It is time to up your game. Be ready to step into your power. Nothing stands in your way besides your own mind and beliefs. Feel the freedom of the future you're creating for yourself. Relish your new life and light."

Along with this feeling of freedom comes the knowing that I am supported as I move into this next chapter of my life, which is also connected to the accelerated, expanding consciousness of our human collective and world. Each one of us can heal and transform by opening up to the power of love and wisdom that is available to us from all aspects of our Earth Community, including the wild animals. In turn, we can reciprocate with our feelings of compassion for her. The ability to recognize her value and need for health and harmony ignites the calling to follow through with appropriate action in her honor. May we all feel moved to be our best selves as we are humbled and graced by the blessings of this amazing planet!

Heather Green has practiced as an intuitive, animal communicator, and energy healer for humans and animals since 2009. She channels messages from the Pleiadian High Council, Angels of the Elohim, and animal and nature collectives to assist others with navigating their lives during these times of accelerated change. In 2013, Heather authored *For the Love of Horses: An Animal Communicator's Guide to Helping Our Horses and Healing Our Lives.*

www.tealhealing.com

A Quest for Belonging that Brought Me Home

By Catheryne Harsh

What is Community to me?

Well...
We're in One
Whether we recognize it or not.
Every individual decision made
Has shaped the collective experience of
The Present Now.

Even amidst solitary adventure,
I am inextricably linked
With the intricate web of Intelligence
Inhabiting countless forms
Of unique Expressions
Across time and space.

I say this as someone
Who has walked solo
For long stretches of my life.
Even during bouts of partnership
And cosmic encounters with
Sages, wizards, teachers, friends,

The siren call of my Soul
Consistently drew me forward
On a road less traveled.
It's been a narrow path,
One that disregards
Instinctual desires for stability found
Within concretized "community."

Perhaps this sounds cynical—
I mean no disrespect!
I've simultaneously craved and rejected
Such structure for decades…
The proverbial bird
Flying from nest to nest asking,
"Are you my Mother?"

I see Community
As a system of roots;
Information, nutrition, emotion…energy
Flowing throughout the network
With intention of its own,
Ignoring human definitions of
Mine, yours, ours.
At some points
These roots converge in heavy clusters,
Deeply intertwined and
Unavoidably aware of their interdependence.
At other points
Roots shoot off in independent investigations,
Daring voyages of solitary probing into the Unknown…
Yet even then,
They are mere extensions
Of the Web of Life
In which we all participate.

To say connection to Community
Ends when the root tip
Perceives itself surrounded by Earth alone
Is a limited perspective.

Community is like any other
Aspect of Existence;
It's there to help you,
And to reflect you,
But not to fill you.

How many times have I knocked
On the door of a shiny new
Teacher, lover, friend, *community*…
Extending my cup,
Begging for something
Outside of mySelf
To fill it;
"Make me feel whole"
"Show me I'm worthy"
"Distract me from the gnawing emptiness I feel inside."
It's called co-dependence
(Very different from interdependence);
And while there's a place
For external validation
(And encouragement for sure)
On our journey of Remembrance,
It's food for newborns
And the milk sours quickly.

Mature community
Is a collection
Of overflowing cups,
Where the Light within me
Honors the Light within you,

But each individual takes complete
Responsibility for their own Light;
Neediness has transformed into Sovereignty
And exchanges between members
Are charged with
Unconditional Love.
It's holding
Another Being or a
Particular configuration of Beings
With an open hand—
Understanding the dynamic nature of Life
And that True Peace is sourced internally.

Mature *community* says:
"I love you and know we are connected
Beyond what intellectually makes sense.
Therefore, I trust you and your physical presence
To a Divine Plan greater than my own.
Regardless of whether you stay or go,
I bless you on your journey
And will rejoice if we have the
Opportunity to dance again...
But I don't own your time,
Or require your presence
To feel complete."

That being said,
We are having a human experience,
And other humans are often catalysts
In the process of awakening
To the Truth of who we are.

I could wax eloquently
About the times my Soul
Caught fire

Through proximity
To another's Presence-
Serving as:
Activator,
Initiator,
Guide,
Midwife-
Helping me birth something
New within my Being.

How my heart burns
With love and gratitude for these individuals
Who's authentic expressions
Were manna in the desert when
I thought I was starving for
Truth. Love. Connection.
In retrospect,
I See
These Divine Co-creators were
Living out their unique destiny
Which played a perfect part in my
Personal story of Remembrance.

They watered a seed
And fanned a flame,
Mirroring an aspect of mySelf
That desired nurturing-
For no one can teach you something new;
They merely reveal what was inside the entire time.

I have also experienced *community*
That left me wanting...
Countless times when I didn't receive
The love, affirmation, belonging

I was seeking.
This too was perfect for my Soul's evolution.
It's not that Community was broken;
It's that I was trying to heal my hemorrhaging heart
With the band-aid of other people's love.
No matter how beautiful the bandage,
It wasn't equipped for the task at hand.

Once we stop searching
For a fantastical *community*
To fix us,
Or provide permanence and predictability,
We are then able to experience utter
Gladness and Joyful Communion
In each encounter with
Beings from every walk of life.

Once we relinquish the profile
Of the perfect pool of people
Who we perceive will relieve us
From the fear and heaviness within,
We then enjoy true relationship—
One that seeks nothing,
Gives without agenda,
And thus receives everything.

Once our addiction to external validation ceases,
And we've renounced the ruse of "belonging,"
We are then free to experience Love
In all its varied forms;
We see Beauty
In the breathtaking diversity of all life-based interactions.
We feel kinship with the mailman
Are inspired by the taxi driver

Fall in love with the citrus farmer
Learn from the trees
Are humbled by the elements
Flirt with the flowers—

When we have learned to nurture our own heart,
Then the most unlikely friendships
Offer the most surprising nectar;
We are finally available to celebrate
Community directly in front of us
Rather than holding our breath
For an idealized collection of Beings
Somewhere out there in the future.

In my opinion,
Life is enhanced
When shared.
We are all unique aspects of
All That There Is…
Individual fractals
Of a diamond beyond our wildest imagination.
We embody the great paradox:
Separate experiences
Of the One Living Presence.

And on this plane,
We have much to do together-
Gifts desire to be given,
Love wants to be offered.
Laughter, stories, art, play, music, discovery…
Are all joys to experience
In Community.
But until we source
Our joy, contentment and happiness
From the True Source,

Community may more often than not
Draw us in
To remind our hearts
That nothing outside of the Eternal, Divine
Christed Light dwelling within,
Will quench our thirst
And satisfy the longing
Our Soul craves.

I n this current cycle of life, **Catheryne Harsh** finds herSelf deeply focused on the alchemical process of *being* rather than *doing*. Professionally, her *doing* was with non-profits, technology, entrepreneurship, philanthropy, and consulting. However, Catheryne's intrigue with travel, nature, sacred currencies, and wisdom traditions has contributed to the growth and evolution of her inner *being*. As an anchor of Divine Feminine Love on this planet, she currently lives in Bozeman, Montana, where she's grounding into the strength of the Rockies while working on her first book. Catheryne.harsh@gmail.com

Conclusion –
We Are All Connected

In this book, I use the word *tribe* interchangeably with *community*, meaning a group or a collective that shares a sense of unity or purpose. Whether it's an organized social, familial or professional community; a group of individuals, either neighbors or anonymous strangers; representatives from the natural world, perhaps trees or a pod of whales; or more transcendent abstractions such as a universal source or philosophy. The writers in this book have been supported and uplifted out of their darkest moments by one or more of these tribes.

Each of these stories takes us to the brink of depletion. Ultimately, however, these are tales of resiliency. The authors reveal their wounds with a tender reflection that also mirrors our own. Although these accomplished women are healers within their respective specialties, it was not foremost in their minds to initially ask for support. Perhaps *independence* carries the shadow or stigma of not being worthy or needing to belong to a tribe and, therefore, feeling like we must heal alone.

Yes, healing can be an individual process, but *interdependence,* in a tribal aspect, adds so much more depth. Perhaps the takeaway here is that during those times when you think that you cannot possibly take one more step, the outreach from a compassionate tribe is a safety net, breaking your fall and showing you that—regardless of your background or circumstances—you are valued.

My intention is—as you vicariously share the journey with these women from the safety of the written page, or if you are in the throes of a physical or existential disruption—that you feel empowered by their experiences to know that *healing is always possible*. A community exponentially expands your access to love. Your tribe might provide longer-lasting or more profound solutions to your challenges, or it could be the equivalent of a group hug, an opportunity to heal by belonging.

Historically, human survival has been enhanced by our extended families, our clans or tribes; essentially, an ecosystem where everyone has had a role that benefits the community at large. Contemporary studies such as the Blue Zones and the Roseto Effect show how family and community support improves health and longevity. Research continues into the importance of social networks, relationships, kindness, conscientiousness, optimism, and volunteerism—factors "that make life better and nicer," according to science journalist Marta Zaraska. "Whereas diet and exercise are important, the social connection and the *soft drivers of health* — how you live your life, mentally, and socially — are even more important."

By the 21st-century, technology vastly expanded our global community, multiplying our options for connection. That is, until 2020, when a microscopic virus instantaneously shifted the paradigm, requiring strict physical boundaries and isolation. Gradually, online tribes cropped up within the rooms of the Zoom video application, stitching us together into new special-interest communities like a virtual game of tic-tac-toe.

There is no doubt that we are most powerful when we share common values and interests. We have our smaller tribes or communities, but we are now realizing that humankind is ONE tribe!

A bond is formed between people sharing a common experience— whether emotional, physical, mental or spiritual—that draws them into a moment of intimacy, regardless of who is giving or receiving. Whatever your circumstances, as you close this book, I want to leave you feeling a renewed sense of hope and reconnection to yourself, to others, to the planet and to your divinity, with increased self-awareness and consciousness as you move forward as a shining light.

QUESTIONS TO ASK YOURSELF

1. Can you think of times when your community has made a difference in your life?
2. List the ways your community has supported you. How has this support inspired, impacted or shifted your life?
3. Have you witnessed your community supporting others? How does that make you feel?
4. Have you ever been part of a community that changed someone else's life?
5. How do you "recognize" your tribe?
6. Can we all be ONE tribe? Your thoughts.